Becoming God's
Faithful Armor Bearer

Patty Handly

BALBOA.
PRESS
A DIVISION OF HAY HOUSE

Scripture taken from the Amplified Bible, copyright © 1954, 1958, 1962, 1964, 1965, 1987 by The Lockman Foundation. Used by permission.

All Scripture quotations in this publications are from The Message. Copyright © by Eugene H. Peterson 1993, 1994, 1995, 1996, 2000, 2001, 2002. Used by permission of NavPress Publishing Group.

Scripture taken from the New King James Version. Copyright © 1979, 1980, 1982 by Thomas Nelson, Inc. Used by permission. All rights reserved. Scripture taken from the King James Version of the Bible.

Balboa Press books may be ordered through booksellers or by contacting:

Balboa Press
A Division of Hay House
1663 Liberty Drive
Bloomington, IN 47403
www.balboapress.com
1 (877) 407-4847

Because of the dynamic nature of the Internet, any web addresses or links contained in this book may have changed since publication and may no longer be valid. The views expressed in this work are solely those of the author and do not necessarily reflect the views of the publisher, and the publisher hereby disclaims any responsibility for them.

The author of this book does not dispense medical advice or prescribe the use of any technique as a form of treatment for physical, emotional, or medical problems without the advice of a physician, either directly or indirectly. The intent of the author is only to offer information of a general nature to help you in your quest for emotional and spiritual well-being. In the event you use any of the information in this book for yourself, which is your constitutional right, the author and the publisher assume no responsibility for your actions.

Any people depicted in stock imagery provided by Thinkstock are models, and such images are being used for illustrative purposes only. Certain stock imagery © Thinkstock.

Print information available on the last page.

ISBN: 978-1-5043-5081-5 (sc)
ISBN: 978-1-5043-5082-2 (hc)
ISBN: 978-1-5043-5080-8 (e)

Library of Congress Control Number: 2016902557

Balboa Press rev. date: 2/25/2016

Contents

Preface

BLESSED! BLESSED! BLESSED!

How would you feel if you knew you could be blessed every single day of your life? Would that bring you joy? Would you wake up every morning with great anticipation of what your day would look like? Would you go to sleep with the same expectations you held as a child on Christmas Eve after seeing all the presents under the tree?

THE GREAT NEWS IS YOU CAN BE BLESSED EVERY DAY OF YOUR LIFE! **THE GREATER NEWS IS** <u>YOU CAN BE A BLESSING EVERY SINGLE DAY OF YOUR LIFE</u>! It isn't dependent upon anyone BUT YOU.

Would you like to be overwhelmed with the favor and blessings of God? Now, I'm not talking about the blessings that come from sheer obedience. I'm talking about the *extreme, uncommon, magnificent, ridiculous blessings* that come to you because you have chosen to be an on purpose blessing to everyone you come in contact with "every single day of your life." You have set the needs of others before your own needs, and you are determined to serve, rather than to be served, "ON PURPOSE".

[Sounds familiar, doesn't it?]

Jesus said, in Matthew 20:26b-28 Amplified (AMP)

"but whoever desires to become great among you, let him be your servant. [27] And whoever desires to be first among you, let him be your slave— [28]just as the Son of Man did not come to be served, but to serve, and to give His life as a ransom for many."

I pray when you have completed this book you will have made the second best decision of your life, and that my friend, is to live "on purpose" as a blessing, as a servant and as a friend *to all*.

[The first and best decision of your life, of course, was your decision to receive Jesus into your heart and invite Him to be your Lord and Savior.]

Introduction

Since I began writing this book, I have faced great challenges and intense change in almost every area of my life. I have been forced through adversity to make hard decisions and to face the consequences of those decisions. Nevertheless, I have persevered to complete this work. I am convinced more than ever that this book will reach hundreds of thousands of people, just like you, who desire to serve God, His church, and His people with all their hearts, souls, minds and strength.

Throughout my life, especially in these past few years, I have given the Lord many opportunities to teach me, and to raise me up, (or should I say, to lower me or humble me) through His correction and life's changes in order that I could truly know His heart and His will concerning me. It has been through such adversity, that I have come to know God's great faithfulness, and His greater plan for my life.

I pray as you read this book, you will learn through mistakes I have made and challenges I have faced, in order that you may bypass some of the obstacles that slowed my progress and oftentimes discouraged me a little longer than need be. I pray this book will bless you, encourage you, and strengthen you to **become God's faithful armor bearer**.

[Please note, throughout this work, I will refer to the armor bearer as "he," but this is only for the simplicity of reading. I believe God has called every person, (male and female) to be His armor bearer.]

What is an Armor Bearer?

When I began discussing this book with a publishing agent, I was surprised when she asked me, "What is an armor bearer?" I was shocked, as a Christian, she was unaware of the term. I did my best to explain it, as I quoted excerpts from my book and gave a few examples. She became excited as I shared, and I became even more determined to get this book completed and into the hands of so many who truly desire to serve our Lord, and one another.

In researching the few materials available, I discovered many Christians have varying ideas about what an armor bearer is, or what an armor bearer should be. Sadly to me, this subject is not taught very much from the pulpit. Or, at least that has been my experience for over 30 years of attending Christian church. It is truly no surprise to me that so many are unfamiliar and/or confused on the subject and role of the armor bearer. Depending on who you speak with, the subject of armor bearer can be negative, while for others, like me, it is exciting and quite honestly, exuberant.

One evening I came across an article, or blog, that grabbed my attention and pulled at my heartstrings. The host shared, there is **no office** of armor bearer mentioned in the Bible.

While I believe the office of armor bearer is more "implied" than stated, we can rest assured, the role of the armor bearer is still quite vital to the work of the ministry.

[I truly believe you don't need an office to hold the position of the armor bearer]

I sat and read hours of conversations of people sharing their thoughts on the subject of "the armor bearer." I struggled with much of the content, and the negativity, but I felt it was important to continue through the end to get a real feel for the subject, and man's conviction on the matter.

One particular article suggested that Pastor's with armor bearers are overbearing and manipulative. It also suggested that <u>ALL</u> armor bearers are striving for position and attention. It seemed very negative and obviously dishonoring to both Pastors and armor bearers alike.

While I prefer to believe that is not the norm, I do believe we, as armor bearers, must be aware of the danger in stepping into this trap. So, the question remains; What is an armor bearer? Here are just a few of the negative statements or opinions I gathered from my research to describe an armor bearer.

[Sarcasm is intentional]

"that guy who is always WITH the Pastor."

"that girl who runs around looking busy all the time."

"that person who is ALWAYS STARING AT EVERYBODY."

"that guy who keeps trying to win kudos from the Pastor and the leadership."

"that person who keeps telling everyone "I AM THE ARMOR BEARER!""

"that pretentious one, who works alongside the Pastor, but is SECRETLY DESIRING THE PASTOR'S POSITION."

"that woman who is in desperate need of attention, who falsely serves, whose intent is only selfish gain"

[As I mentioned, this is what I came away with after doing some research. I am in no way in agreement with these statements, I share them only as a point of reference in my decision to write this book correctly, and with all due diligence]

Instead of asking, WHAT an armor bearer is, perhaps the better question to be asked is, **WHO IS AN ARMOR BEARER?** At least, that is the question I would like to answer, with the Lord's help.

"Being an armor bearer isn't always comfortable, it doesn't always feel good. Being an armor bearer doesn't mean your friends or family, IT MEANS, you're faithful. It means you care. It means you're there! Being an armor bearer means you're loyal, dependable, reliable, trustworthy, loving and jealous for the honor that is due the subject of interest."

Patty Handly

"Who" is an Armor Bearer?

Truly, the title or "the position" (of the armor bearer) is NOT as important as "the posture" of the armor bearer. Is his position one of "climbing over" someone, or one of laying himself down for Someone? Is his goal to reach a higher pinnacle, or is his position/posture/attitude, one of humility and honor? In other words, does he humble himself before the Lord in order to pray and seek God for His counsel concerning serving and ministering to the needs of others, or is his service to others simply a means to an end? (his plans, his ambitions, his agenda?)

With permission, I'd like to share part of a message preached one Sunday at my church awhile back. This message was part of a series entitled "The Assignment, the Anointing and the adversary" (no, he, the adversary, doesn't deserve a capitol letter)

"Being an armor bearer isn't always comfortable, it doesn't always feel good. Being an armor bearer doesn't mean your friends or family, IT MEANS, you're faithful. It means you care. It means you're there! Being an armor bearer means you're loyal, dependable, reliable, trustworthy, loving and jealous for the honor that is due the subject of interest."

Patty Handly

The Team Player vs. The Pretender

The title to this particular message in this series was, "A Team Player vs. a Pretender."

It may seem an obvious thing, to desire to be a team player on the Lord's team, right? After all, we all know He ALWAYS WINS!! I agree with my Pastor, "The problem arises when we no longer desire to hear, or listen to the team Captain for instructions." This occurs when WE begin to desire TO BE the TEAM CAPTAIN, or, the TEAM LEADER; THE ONE "making the calls" instead of the one receiving the calls". At Soul Harvest Worship Center, we call that, "being all large and in charge" or having an "all that and a bag of chips" attitude.

Pastor shared that a team player (whom I liken to an armor bearer), is willing to give up their position for the mission, while the pretender is willing to abandon the mission for the position, (the position he is striving for). For example, it may be advantageous to the team for you, or me, to sit this inning out. Sure, nobody enjoys warming the bench, but I can tell you from experience, "the bench" may be the best place for us at that time (or for that whole season).

When I was in High School, my basketball coach began sitting me out while all the rest of the team seemed to have opportunity to play in the game. I was in complete denial that that was " best for the team" and I sulked and sulked until I finally told the coach "I QUIT!!," to which he unbelievably responded, "But I need a bench Handly."

Wow! Nice going coach! Did he not understand how sensitive I was at this juncture of my life? Well, the funny thing is, the team successfully won more and more games <u>without me</u>. The truth is, no one really seemed to miss me, and life on the court continued.

If I were a true team player, I would have continued to be a part of the team. I would have continued to participate, (showing up for practices) and I would have sat on that bench every single game and cheered my team on. I would have given them my time and my support, and not behaved as I did. I obviously was NOT a team player at all.

I'll say it again, the team player is always willing to do whatever is necessary for the sake of the team's success, while the pretender is willing to do everything necessary for HIS OWN success, REGARDLESS of how it effects the team!

In my example, my true colors showed immediately when I abandoned the team because I did not truly care about the team's success. I cared only about myself being on the court, with the ball. <u>I just wanted to play</u>!

My Pastor continued to share that while it may be difficult to recognize the pretender right away, (since he wears the same uniform and acts the part of the team player) he is quickly identified when he is called upon to serve the needs of the team. As I shared in my example, I was not.

Depending on how good a pretender he is, it may take a little longer to recognize him; but time will always reveal his true colors, because a pretender cannot pretend forever.

Within a church setting, an effective tool in identifying pretenders from true team players is to ask them "to serve." I think asking anyone to serve the church scrubbing toilets after a Christmas or Easter service, or after any big event is a sure fire way to see into the heart of a person. Even if a person agrees to serve, he will still be identified as a team player or a pretender by the way he serves."

It always breaks my heart to see someone serve who makes it obvious he is not serving with a grateful heart. Or, on the other hand, there is the one who serves but has to announce to the whole world that he has just spent such and such amount of time, "serving the church" instead of keeping it secret. I think of the following Scriptures when I think about serving. Although they may be written about giving, praying, and fasting, I still believe they are relevant to serving.

Matthew 6:4 King James Version (KJV)

"That thine alms may be in secret: and thy Father which seethin secret himself shall reward thee openly."

Matthew 6:6 King James Version (KJV)

"But thou, when thou prayest, enter into thy closet, and when thou hast shut thy door, pray to thy Father which is in secret; and thy Father which seeth in secret shall reward thee openly."

Matthew 6:18 King James Version (KJV)

"That thou appear not unto men to fast, but unto thy Father which is in secret: and thy Father, which seeth in secret, shall reward thee openly."

A team player will scrub the toilets in complete joy, singing praises, or praying, or just having fun, enjoying the task at hand, while the pretender will do everything in his power to get out of the task. I think of the child who does an intentionally bad job on a household chore, thinking he will not be asked to do this chore again. But the wise parent is aware of this tactic and quickly shows the child that perhaps "more practice in this chore will make him better at it." Next time the child does the job, he is indeed much better at it and he is spared the extra practice.

[Pretenders are quick with excuses and reasons why they are unable to serve, or unavailable for that duty. If this is a pattern you recognize, you may consider it a sign, that their heart is truly not one of a team player or one of a true armor bearer.]

The True Armor Bearer

The armor bearer is mentioned in the first book ever published, the Holy Bible. In the Bible he is described very clearly as "the servant to" the King. For the purposes of this book, in this 21st century, we will consider the various roles of the armor bearer. Firstly, and most importantly, the armor bearer is to be the servant to the KING of kings and Lord of lords, Jesus Christ. Secondly, the armor bearer is to be the servant to the Pastor. Keep in mind, when we serve the Pastor, we are also serving the local church, and the congregation. The whole intent of this book is to encourage YOU to begin (or continue) to serve your Pastor, and to teach you "as we serve our Pastors, we are indeed serving and ministering to our Lord Himself."

Matthew 25:40 King James Version (KJV)

"And the King shall answer and say unto them, 'Verily I say unto you, "in so much as you have done unto one of the least of these my brethren, you have done unto Me."'"

The Bible also refers to the armor bearer as the "cup bearer". The cup bearer would drink from the cup presented to the King in the event that someone had poisoned it. Thus, the cup bearer demonstrated his love and faithfulness, (his duty) in his willingness to give his life for the sake of the King. THAT IS WHAT CUP BEARERS DO.

In a more modern, or secular description, the armor bearer can be likened to the secret service agent who runs beside the motorcade serving protection detail to the President of the United States of America. In this example, the agent jumps in the line of fire and takes the bullet meant for the Commander and Chief, thus giving his life in service for the President. While this may seem an unreasonable expectation, the agent himself takes this position very seriously and makes no compromise for the job "he has chosen" as a career. His heart is one of great service and sacrifice, much like that of the armor bearer.

On March 30, 1981 Secret Service Agent Tim McCarthy threw up his arms and spread his body to shield President Ronald Regan from the shooter who attempted his assassination, thus taking a bullet in the chest for the POTUS. He demonstrated his willingness to make the sacrifice to jump in harm's way, to be willing to give his own life for another. Although Agent McCarthy did not consider himself a hero, rather, he stated in many interviews, he did what he was trained to do, to put the life of the President above his own.

I purposefully use Agent McCarthy as an example for several reasons, one being the obvious, that he is a great example. But the real reason I choose to include Agent McCarthy is this. When I think about the assassination attempt on President Regan, I first think about President Regan, then, I think about Press Secretary James Brady, and only now, have I ever even thought about Secret Service Agent, Tim McCarthy. To be honest, I had to look up his name on the Internet because I didn't even know his name. As a matter of fact, I have never even thought about Agent Tim McCarthy until the writing of this book. You see, Tim McCarthy was not the subject of interest; President Ronald Regan was the subject of interest.

I bet if we asked anyone to remember that day and that newscast, most of us would think first about Mr. James Brady. Brady was shot in the head because he was in such close proximity to the President, while Agent McCarthy INTENTIONALLY put himself in harm's way for the purpose of taking the bullet for the President.

In each of these examples, we see the true armor bearer as the one who always puts the King, the President, the Pastor, or 'the OTHER' before himself. The true armor bearer **purposefully** chooses to put his personal vision second to the vision of the Pastor, in order to run with another's vision over his own. He chooses to be second, third or sometimes even last, in order that the needs of others are met first. He chooses to be unseen. Even if he is noticed, he <u>chooses not to notice</u>. That is what makes him a TRUE armor bearer.

[Please keep in mind I am not saying the armor bearer is to put his family or spouse on hold habitually while he is out serving the needs of others. God forbid! The Bible is careful to instruct us on this matter]

We read in 1 Timothy 3:1-13 Paul's instructions to Timothy …

1 Timothy 3:1-13 (NKJV)

Qualifications of Overseers

3 This is a faithful saying: If a man desires the position of a bishop,[a] he desires a good work. ² A bishop then must be blameless, the husband of one wife, temperate, sober-minded, of good behavior, hospitable, able to teach; ³ not given to wine, not violent, not greedy for money,[b] but gentle, not quarrelsome, not covetous; ⁴ one who rules his own house well, having his children in submission with all reverence ⁵ (for if a man does not know how to rule his own house, how will he take care of the church of God?); ⁶ not a novice, lest being puffed up with pride he fall into the same condemnation as the devil. ⁷ Moreover he must have a good testimony among those who are outside, lest he fall into reproach and the snare of the devil.

Qualifications of Deacons

⁸ Likewise deacons must be reverent, not double-tongued, not given to much wine, not greedy for money, ⁹ holding the mystery of the faith with a pure conscience. ¹⁰ But let these also first be tested; then let them serve as deacons, being found blameless. ¹¹ Likewise, their wives must be reverent, not slanderers, temperate, faithful in all things. ¹² Let deacons be the husbands of one wife, ruling their children and their own houses well. ¹³ For those who have served well as deacons obtain for themselves a good standing and great boldness in the faith which is in Christ Jesus.

[A good Pastor will teach these tools of leadership, a great Pastor will demand they be followed. I am thankful to have a GREAT Pastor, who teaches the priority of family over ministry]

"Being an armor bearer isn't always comfortable, it doesn't always feel good. Being an armor bearer doesn't mean your friends or family, IT MEANS, you're faithful. It means you care. It means you're there! Being an armor bearer means you're loyal, dependable, reliable, trustworthy, loving and jealous for the honor that is due the subject of interest."

Patty Handly

The Position of the Armor Bearer

My Pastor said it right, "The position of the team player is on his knees." This indeed is the position of the true armor bearer. It is the place we are serving and giving our best.

I believe when we are on our <u>knees</u>, and not on our <u>needs</u>, we will serve our Pastors, congregations and our Lord best, with the true spirit of humility. That is exactly how we should serve.

The true armor bearer is faithful to prayer lifting the needs of the Pastor, the staff, the leadership, the ministry teams, and the congregation before the Lord. He is diligent to keep himself in prayer and in that spirit of humility in order to serve in integrity and righteousness. (God's righteousness and not our own, lest we boast in ourselves)

[When we walk in His righteousness, we have the audience of heaven.]

The Bible speaks of the prayers of a righteous in the book of James.

James 5:15-17 New King James Version (NKJV)

[15] And the prayer of faith will save the sick, and the Lord will raise him up. And if he has committed sins, he will be forgiven. [16] Confess your trespasses to one another, and pray for one another, that you may be healed. THE EFFECTIVE, FERVENT PRAYER OF A RIGHTEOUS MAN AVAILETH MUCH"

The armor bearer must also be willing to bear the armor and the burden of the Pastor. HE SHOULD NEVER INTEND TO MAKE THE LOAD (BURDEN) HEAVIER!! He should never desire to add more to the Pastor's plate. Rather, his desire should be to aid the Pastor and <u>lighten</u> the load. This true armor bearer desires to assist the Pastor in finishing the race, not in running the race for the Pastor, and certainly not in trampling over the Pastor, in the process.

While the armor bearer may be the one who is usually alongside the Pastor, he is never to lead the Pastor. He should never desire anything more, than to serve, NOT REPLACE, the Pastor.

You see, the armor bearer IS NOT the subject of interest, rather, he is "the faithful servant to" the subject of interest. We saw this in the example of Secret Service Agent, Tim McCarthy. Most people don't even know his name, and yet, he was the one accredited to saving the life of President Ronald Regan.

If the armor bearer is blessed by God with an anointed God led Pastor, he will have the privilege to grow as he serves. He will never fall by the wayside because he is discouraged, misunderstood, or just plain ignorant, UNLESS, he is unwilling to await his appointed time of promotion. In which case, he may leave prematurely, perhaps right before the Lord promotes him. (Once again, I am writing from experience)

"Being an armor bearer isn't always comfortable, it doesn't always feel good. Being an armor bearer doesn't mean your friends or family, IT MEANS, you're faithful. It means you care. It means you're there! Being an armor bearer means you're loyal, dependable, reliable, trustworthy, loving and jealous for the honor that is due the subject of interest."

Patty Handly

The First Armor Bearer

Once upon a time there was a perfect heaven and a perfect earth until sin reared its ugly head. This, my friend, happened in heaven. Yes! Sin, began IN HEAVEN. There was an angel in heaven named Lucifer. He was created by God for one purpose alone. Lucifer was created to bring worship to the throne room of heaven. In Ezekiel 28, vs. 13, we read how Lucifer was formed as an instrument of worship; made of timbrels and pipe. Timbrels are a type of tambourine.

I can only imagine the pipe portion of Lucifer sounding much like a harp or some kind of amplification of a stringed instrument. **He literally was music!** As his body moved through the atmosphere of heaven, I can by faith, hear the sounds of pure adoration and exuberant praise pouring forth unto the Darling of heaven, Jesus, the Christ. Can you hear it? Just think, Lucifer was IN HIS SPOT doing exactly what he was created to do, with the perfect anointing of God to bring forth precisely the ministry he was created for, with everything he needed inside of him. EVERYTHING WAS PERFECT. HE WAS PERFECT.

FOR JUST A MINUTE.. ... FORGET that you know the outcome of Lucifer. **Forget** the fact that you hate him and what he brought to this earth with his sin. **Now**, read the story of how he was created, designed and appointed with a purpose and a plan **AND** with the blessing of God Almighty. (Seriously, forget everything you know about your enemy, the devil, and read this description of how God created and ordained the first armor bearer, the armor bearer to heaven's throne)

Ezekiel 28:12-15 (NKJV) gives a true description of Lucifer

12 "son of man, take up a lamentation for the king of Tyre, and say to him, 'Thus says the Lord God: "you were the seal of perfection, full of wisdom and perfect in beauty. 13 you were in Eden, the garden of God; every precious stone was your covering: The sardius, topaz, and diamond, beryl, onyx, and jasper, sapphire, turquoise, and emerald with gold. The workmanship of your timbrels and pipe was prepared for you on the day you were created. 14 "You were the anointed cherub who covers; I established you; you were on the holy mountain of God; you walked back and forth in the midst of fiery stones. 15 you were perfect in your ways from the day you were created, till iniquity was found in you.

WOW! Imagine that!! Lucifer was perfect in beauty and in purpose, in every way, since the day he was created!! This description, with all the jewels and gems and the workmanship simply blows me away. Heaven, simply heaven.

BUT, Lucifer began to have a change of heart. He became puffed up, and his desires changed. No longer was he happy or content to be the worshiper, but now, he longed to be THE

WORSHIPPED!! He began to lust for the attention and the praise of others. Because of this decision, he was ensnared by the sin of pride and he was cast out of heaven, and denied God's original purpose for his life. Lost forever was the position of honor and the mantle that God had so freely placed upon him. Tragic, simply tragic.

Ezekiel 28:16-19 tells of the heartbreaking story of the fall of the son of man, Lucifer. I say heartbreaking because God's purposes were not fulfilled in this servant. Keep in mind, this happened in heaven and this tragedy spread throughout the entire world.

[This is where I would caution each of us, to take heed.]

Ezekiel 28:16-19 New King James Version (NKJV)

16 "By the abundance of your trading you became filled with violence within, and you sinned, therefore I cast you as a profane thing out of the mountain of God; and I destroyed you, O covering cherub, from the midst of the fiery stones. 17 "your heart was lifted up because of your beauty; you corrupted your wisdom for the sake of your splendor; I cast you to the ground, I laid you before kings, that they might gaze at you. 18 "you defiled your sanctuaries by the multitude of your iniquities, by the iniquity of your trading; therefore I brought fire from your midst; it devoured you, and I turned you to ashes upon the earth in the sight of all who saw you. 19 All who knew you among the peoples are astonished at you; you have become a horror, and shall be no more forever."""

The Message version tells the story this way ...

Ezekiel 28:15-19 The Message (MSG)

A robe was prepared for you

the same day you were created.

You were the anointed cherub.

I placed you on the mountain of God.

You strolled in magnificence

among the stones of fire.

From the day of your creation

you were sheer perfection ...

and then imperfection—evil!—was detected in you.

In much buying and selling

you turned violent, you sinned!

I threw you, disgraced, off the mountain of God.

I threw you out—you, the anointed angel-cherub.

No more strolling among the gems of fire for you!

Your beauty went to your head.

You corrupted wisdom

by using it to get worldly fame.

I threw you to the ground,

sent you sprawling before an audience of kings

and let them gloat over your demise.

By sin after sin after sin,

by your corrupt ways of doing business,

you defiled your holy places of worship.

So I set a fire around and within you.

It burned you up. I reduced you to ashes.

All anyone sees now

when they look for you is ashes,

a pitiful mound of ashes.

"Being an armor bearer isn't always comfortable, it doesn't always feel good. Being an armor bearer doesn't mean your friends or family, IT MEANS, you're faithful. It means you care. It means you're there! Being an armor bearer means you're loyal, dependable, reliable, trustworthy, loving and jealous for the honor that is due the subject of interest."

Patty Handly

Pride Goeth Before Destruction

The Bible teaches us in Proverbs 16:18 King James Version (KJV)

18 Pride goeth before destruction, and an haughty spirit before a fall.

I believe worship leaders, like the once anointed, appointed cherub in heaven, are created to be armor bearers. Each holds an appointed position to lead souls into the embrace of Almighty God.

Everyone of them has a great responsibility to keep themselves before the Lord, only seeking His gaze, and not the gaze of men or mankind. It is a fierce battle for the worshipper to engage. After all, they have replaced Lucifer's position of honor and they now stand on the "mountain of God" as they carry the anointing to bring worship and adoration before the throne room of heaven. (satan hates the worshipper. he is jealous, envious and enraged by the worshipper, who we all know, took his position after he gave it up)

I say to all who will listen, beware of the "platform or the altar" when it becomes "the stage."

Beware of the <u>position</u> of worship leader, without the position of humility and honor. Be sure to give honor to the One and the ONLY ONE who deserves honor. If you have been blessed with the voice of an angel, be sure to use it for the purpose of God's glory alone. satan will come to offer you the wealth of the nations, the glory due only the KING. he will attempt to wow you and entice you and whatever is truly in your heart will ensnare you. Beware, my beloved, beware!

We can use Lucifer's example as a means of escaping the same mistakes he made. I know the spirit of pride would love to destroy every saint's purpose and ultimately destroy every destiny God has ordained for us. Pride did this to Lucifer (who is later called satan) and pride will do the same to us unless we seriously take heed and keep ourselves continually in a place of reverence and humility, acknowledging Christ as our All in All. He is after all, our true destiny.

Read the words in Isaiah and take note of the "I will" statements that Lucifer makes. Observe the pride in his heart as he only acknowledges himself. (I, I, I or as we say in California, "Aye, Aye, Aye")

Isaiah 14:12-14 New King James Version (NKJV)

"How ₁you are fallen from heaven,

O Lucifer, son of the morning!

How you are cut down to the ground,

You who weakened the nations! [13] *For you have said in your heart:*

'I will ascend into heaven,

I will exalt my throne above the stars of God;

I will also sit on the mount of the congregation

On the farthest sides of the north; [14] *I will ascend above the heights of the clouds,*

I will be like the Most High.' [15] *Yet you shall be brought down to Sheol,*

To the lowest depths of the Pit. [16] *"Those who see you will gaze at you,*

And consider you, saying:

'Is this the man who made the earth tremble,

Who shook kingdoms, [17] *Who made the world as a wilderness*

And destroyed its cities,

Who did not open the house of his prisoners?' [18] *"All the kings of the nations,*

All of them, sleep in glory,

Everyone in his own house; [19] *But you are cast out of your grave*

Like an abominable branch,

Like the garment of those who are slain,

Thrust through with a sword,

Who go down to the stones of the pit,

Like a corpse trodden underfoot.

[This is indeed a terrible truth that must be remembered and never forgotten. I pray if you take anything from this book, you will take this truth with you forever]

Lead Us Not Into Temptation

The greatest temptation of the armor bearer is to get our focus off the True Subject, the LORD Himself. We are at risk of being cast out of our destiny, as well as being removed from the position of honor that comes from being an armor bearer when we willfully allow ourselves to become our own object of affection. The Lord created us to worship Him, not man, not woman, not ourselves, but Him alone. (We saw this example with Lucifer)

When we esteem others higher than ourselves, we honor the Lord, for that is what He commands us to do. But, we MUST NEVER esteem anyone, ESPECIALLY ourselves, higher than the Lord. God forbid!

Jesus said in Luke 10:18

"I saw satan fall like lightening from heaven."

In Revelation 12:9b, John writes

"he was cast to the earth and his angels were cast out with him."

Although satan arrived upon this earth with "his personal sin," it wasn't long before he spread that sin to all mankind. But, God took care of that too.

We know this because the Bible declares in John 3:16-17

"For God so loved the world that He gave His only begotten Son, that whosoever believes in Him shall have everlasting life. For God did not come to condemn the world, but that, through HIM man would be saved."

[You see, the Lord does not want to send us where we deserve to go, He wants to bless us, and send us where HE desires us to be, which is, with Him, in His presence. He wants to bless us, with purpose and He wants to bless us on purpose!]

Becoming an "On Purpose" Blessing

Originally, I had titled this book, <u>Becoming An on Purpose Blessing</u> for truly that is the heart of its message. This book spent a few years sitting on the shelf, partially written, partially covered in dust. Then one day the Lord clearly challenged me to pick it up and begin writing again. He further instructed me to change the title to <u>Becoming God's Faithful Armor Bearer</u> .

From that moment, I knew I had God's blessing to continue to write, and I believed this was indeed a work the Lord wanted me to complete. Now as I typed, the Lord began to download ideas and information almost faster than my fingers could move across the keyboard. He began to share specific details and past experiences He wanted me to include in this obviously incomplete work I now held in my hand.

My response to Him again was, "Yes Lord, do whatsoever You will with this book. It is Yours!! Unless You write it, I know it will never accomplish <u>ALL</u> You desire it to accomplish."

It is my prayer, that when you have finished reading this book you will become a person intent upon blessing every person you encounter every day of your life, <u>for the rest of your life</u>.

The Pen of the Ready Writer

I was once a long way off. Like the prodigal son we read about in the Gospel of Luke, I too, had once lived in the Father's house, celebrated life and knew His love. But, I also walked away from His purpose and destiny. After many years, I returned to His house and was met with great love and support much like the prodigal son.

Shortly after my return to my Father's house, my Pastor encouraged me when she said, "You are the pen of the ready writer." That inspired me, to say the least. I thought she meant that my "writing was timely, or perhaps on target. You know, 'inspired." Since I am a poet, I would oftentimes write poems and include them with my daily emails. I was touched to think or believe that I was the pen of the ready writer.

As I grew more deeply in the Word, I was blessed to learn the "ready writers" were those whom (if I understand correctly) oftentimes, transcribed the manuscripts in the Bible for the actual authors. For example, I believe Qoheleth, transcribed the book of Ecclesiastes for King Solomon. I know the words belong to Solomon, but, the pen of the ready writer, I believe was in fact Qoheleth, (the Preacher).

Psalm 45:1 King James Version (KJV)

45 My heart is inditing a good matter: I speak of the things which I have made touching the king: my tongue is the pen of a ready writer.

Can you imagine how amazing it would have been to have experienced personally Jesus teaching His disciples or listening to Paul preach his sermons, being present as Moses separated the great sea? Okay, maybe not that one. But you know what I mean, to be present on the hillside, or in the Temple, and to have actually seen the events as they took place. I would have loved to have been the pen of a ready writer back in the day, but I am just as blessed believing I can be one now.

This may be a stretch, but, I believe these so called 'ready writers' in Scripture, were in fact armor bearers. I want to be obedient to obey all the Lord asks of me and one day, I pray I will be so in tune with Him, He won't even have to ask. He will just download a book and I will write it. How He provides the publishing and the distribution will be His job. My job, as always, is to simply be obedient.

Stop, Drop and Roll

As a Christian, and as a writer, I have learned the importance of the almost forgotten lesson from grade school ... STOP, DROP AND ROLL. In school, students were taught if they were ever "on fire" they should stop, drop and roll in order to smother the flames and escape harm. It was and is an important lesson for everyone to know.

As an armor bearer to the Lord, I pray to be obedient to that still small voice of God. That voice that says, "Turn here" or "Speak to that lady, tell her how beautiful she is," "Ask that person if they need help." As a Christian, we should all be "in tune' with the sound of our Daddy's voice. I know growing up, it was important to answer our parents if they were speaking to us. How much more should we take heed to the voice of our heavenly Father.

I am learning, as an armor bearer, it is extremely important that I **STOP** (anything and everything I am thinking about), **DROP** (everything I am doing at that moment), and **ROLL** (with whatsoever God is about to do in or through me). If I fail to listen, and obey, I miss out on the being a person of intentional blessing, I also miss out on the blessing(s) He desires to give me at that very moment in time.

For example, I have received entire poems when I have obeyed God and pulled off the freeway and taken out a pen and pad of paper. Honestly, with absolutely no effort on my part, the Lord Himself has written the most beautiful poems, stories and songs, simply through my obedience to stop, drop and roll. I hope in reading this portion of the book you will remember to stop, drop and roll when you hear the leading of the Holy Spirit.

[I am thankful to have learned this lesson at school at such a young age, so that the Lord could use this lesson now in this book. But, as far as being on fire goes, I believe now, I would prefer the LORD set me on fire, to burn for His glory, (with the fire of His Spirit, and not actual earthly flames of fire) Amen]

His Name Was Charlie

I'd like to share a life changing event I experienced that forever changed my way of living. I pray it will bless you and perhaps encourage you in some way. It is a long story, but I pray you will be smiling at the end.

One evening I was pulling onto the street of my church when I saw a couple walking from the bus stop onto the church property. I had never seen or recognized this couple, but I felt drawn to them as I watched them approach the steps to my church. Throughout the service I kept seeing them, wondering why I was so interested in them. (I sat in the choir loft on the platform of the church, so the congregation was before me) After service, I saw them sitting on the bench awaiting the bus. Since this was a special Christmas service, we ran late. I was quite certain no buses would be running at this late hour, I offered them a ride home. They admitted they lived a far distance from the church, but I did not mind, after all, what would Jesus do?

We had been driving a bit with minimal conversation, since they were very quiet and we were in all actuality complete strangers. We were practically the only ones on the road this night, which is extremely odd for San Jose. As a matter of fact, there was only one other car on the road, about a car's distance in front of us. All of a sudden, it looked as if the car in front of us hit a jaywalker. The car immediately stopped and the man fell to the ground. I stopped my car, jumped out to see what had happened. The young man was covered in blood, I was sure the car next to me had hit him. I asked him "Do you know Jesus?" and he said, "yes."

About this time the driver came out of his car and asked me, "Did you just come from Kenny Foreman's church?" to which I replied, "yes, I did."

I continued to speak to the injured man, now lying on the ground in front of this man's car. I asked the man again if he was a Christian and if he had ever received Jesus into his heart, as I feared this man was about to die right in that very moment. He said yes he was a Christian and that his name was Charlie. I said, "You're going to be okay Charlie, God sent me here for you. You're going to be okay. I'm not even supposed to be over here."

Charlie was crying and in great pain. He proceeded to tell me what had happened. He was not struck by the car at all.

Charlie began to describe what had happened to him just moments before our two cars came on the scene. Charlie said, "I was driving my car and this other car kept honking at me, motioning for me to pull over. I finally pulled over, then the guy got out of his car and came to my car door. Another man came to the other side of my car. They opened my car door and began stabbing me over and over again." Charlie's pain was getting worse and he was crying so much it was difficult to understand him. He continued, "then they pulled me out of my car and took off in my car. I started walking, looking for help from someone and I fell down, right here in front of this car."

"You mean, you weren't hit by the car?" I asked. "No," said Charlie. His breathing became increasingly weak as he asked me my name. I told him, "My name is Patty. Charlie, you're going to be okay. God sent me here for you Charlie."

I asked, "May I take a look Charlie." He was covered, soaked in blood, I counted about seven or eight stab wounds, one which was so deep, I could hardly stand to look. I could hear Charlie's breathing becoming weaker and weaker. I put my coat on him and held him in my arms as I said, "Breathe with me Charlie, like they do in Lamaze class. Breathe with me ... slowly, with me." Every once in awhile he would say, "Patty, I'm going to die." I said, "No, Charlie, you are going to live. God sent me here for you. I am not supposed to be here. I know I am here only for you. You are going to live and you are not going to die. Breathe with me Charlie." I sat with my legs on each side of him, holding him to my chest, as tight as I could to try somehow to stop the bleeding from taking his life. It seemed like hours went by, he started to fade in and out as I continued to say, "Charlie, you are going to make it. Don't give up! Breathe with me Charlie, slow steady, shallow breaths."

Finally, the ambulance arrived. They began to work on Charlie, getting him prepped for the drive to the hospital. The driver asked if I wanted to ride in the ambulance. I said,

"Well, I can, but I need to move my car." Then I looked where I had placed my car into "park" and my car was gone. Both cars were gone. There was not a single car on the entire street. The driver of the other car saw my face and came quickly to say, "I moved your car out of the street." I felt a great relief after the rush that came from thinking my car was "gone."

The policeman began taking my statement at the same time the paramedic was preparing Charlie for transport. When the medic overheard me speaking to the officer and realized I did not personally know Charlie, he dismissed me and departed for the hospital. The policeman took more information and asked for my name and number. It was at this moment, I remembered I had two passengers in my car, who were still awaiting a ride home.

If I remember correctly, when I got into my car, my passengers were still sitting in their seats, just as I left them, what seemed so long ago. Honestly, I can't remember any conversation on the way to their home. I only remember thinking and believing in my heart CHARLIE WAS GOING TO BE OKAY.

After dropping off my passengers, I finally arrived at my boyfriend's house to meet his Mother. I was wearing the new beautiful white coat my boyfriend had bought me for Christmas, except now, it was covered with blood. I can only imagine the first impression I made meeting this precious woman of God. My boyfriend was so upset as he opened the door. I hadn't even considered how I looked, wearing my beautiful new coat covered now in blood and dirt from the street. I had put my coat on after getting back into my car. I was cold and it was after all, a nice warm coat. (Funny, I was never cold as I held Charlie in the middle of the street, without my coat)

Our house phone rang a few months later, and my Mother said the call was for me. (Yes, this was in the olden days, before cell phones and household appliances) The conversation went something like this. "Hello." "Hello, my name is Charlie, I don't know if you remem ..."

I quickly interrupted him mid word, "CHARLIE!!! OH MY GOD, CHARLIE. How are you Charlie? How are you?" We talked for awhile, he thanked me for helping him that night. (The policeman had given him my name and phone number) He said he would have died if I had not been there to help him. I said, "Charlie, God sent me there for you! He loves you." I never doubted that Charlie would make a complete recovery, I knew God had sent me to help Charlie that night.

Charlie went on to share how he had been cut in the groan area and should have been unable to walk for the rest of his life, but after several surgeries and months of therapy, he was a miracle!

I was so happy when I hung up the phone, I just cried and cried, knowing, I had paid attention to the Lord, paid attention to the people the Lord was showing me, and arrived at the destination of my assignment, to fulfill the will of God, in saving a man's life. You see, Charlie admitted to me on the phone, he was not living a godly life at the time of his accident, but NOW he was serving the Lord with his life. He was so happy now. You can only imagine how happy that made me feel. I was blessed the Lord allowed this to happen in my first year of being saved. It taught me so much and it still inspires me to listen and obey that still small voice of my Savior.

[Thank You Lord, for Charlie! Thank You Lord that I was attentive and obedient (that night) to stop, drop and roll.]

Becoming Obedient

I have heard it said many times that when you love God, it is easy to obey God. I'll be honest with you, I have loved God most of my life and I have not always been obedient. No matter how much I wanted to be (obedient), I have fallen short, and failed more than I would ever want to admit. I think of Paul's words as I struggle with my own humanity.

Paul writes in Romans 7:15-20 The Message (MSG)

14-16 I can anticipate the response that is coming: "I know that all God's commands are spiritual, but I'm not. Isn't this also your experience?" Yes. I'm full of myself—after all, I've spent a long time in sin's prison. What I don't understand about myself is that I decide one way, but then I act another, doing things I absolutely despise. So if I can't be trusted to figure out what is best for myself and then do it, it becomes obvious that God's command is necessary.

17-20 But I need something more! For if I know the law but still can't keep it, and if the power of sin within me keeps sabotaging my best intentions, I obviously need help! I realize that I don't have what it takes. I can will it, but I can't do it. I decide to do good, but I don't really do it; I decide not to do bad, but then I do it anyway. My decisions, such as they are, don't result in actions. Something has gone wrong deep within me and gets the better of me every time.

Although we may have the greatest intentions, we still may fall into temptation. I remember Peter, as he pleaded with Christ, in the Gospel of Luke. I see the desire in his heart, the love he had for the Master, and yet, his faith failed him.

We read about this in Luke 22:31-34 NKJV

[31] And the Lord said, "Simon, Simon! Indeed, Satan has asked for you, that he may sift you as wheat. [32] But I have prayed for you, that your faith should not fail; and when you have returned to Me, strengthen your brethren."

[33] But he said to Him, "Lord, I am ready to go with You, both to prison and to death."

[34] Then He said, "I tell you, Peter, the rooster shall not crow this day before you will deny three times that you know Me."

Did you notice Jesus did not call his disciple Peter, " Petra, the stone?" Instead, Jesus addressed Peter as Simon. This caught my attention, so I looked up the meaning of Simon and found the name Simon is a variant of a Hebrew name, meaning "**hear, listen**." Now, we modern day Christians may not have realized this, but Peter knew full well, THIS WAS A STRONG WARNING TO HIM. Peter knew his Master was trying to get his attention, both with the use of the name

Simone, and by "repeating the name.." This is the reason Peter was so devastated when he did in fact deny Christ three times before the rooster ever crowed.

[In Scripture, when a word is repeated, especially a name, it is for the purpose of pleading to the EMOTION of the person. For example, when Moses cries out on behalf of his son Isaac, who he is about to sacrifice. Or when Jesus cries out, "Father, Father" as He is on the cross. Here, when Jesus says, "Simone, Simone," He is saying this so Peter will <u>pay attention</u> now, and later, Peter will remember what Jesus said to him and get himself up and move forward.]

I have many times failed to listen or heed the caution of the Lord. I have not always been faithful or obedient, but, I have learned to be more faithful and more obedient by experiencing God's awesome faithfulness in precious moments of (my) surrender. When I stop whatever it is I am currently doing, to listen to the Voice I so dearly love, the voice of my Daddy, the voice of my King. It is then, that I am in complete obedience as my heart wholly surrenders to my Master. This is a testament of His faithfulness and His unwavering patience as He works in me to change my heart, to be a greater reflection of His own heart, not of my own doing, lest I boast in myself. God forbid.

"Being an armor bearer isn't always comfortable, it doesn't always feel good. Being an armor bearer doesn't mean your friends or family, IT MEANS, you're faithful. It means you care. It means you're there! Being an armor bearer means you're loyal, dependable, reliable, trustworthy, loving and jealous for the honor that is due the subject of interest."

Patty Handly

Obedience Wins, Disobedience Loses

I have learned that when I fail to be obedient, I am not the only one who misses out on the blessings of God. <u>Oh yes!!</u> <u>There is always a blessing tied to obedience</u>!!

When I fail to obey the Lord, I not only miss out on the blessing God intended "for me," but, unfortunately, you miss out on the blessing that is intended "for you." You see, we are blessed to be a blessing. God is a big God and as such, He never does small. He never does adequate. He is always doing abundantly more than we could ever ask or think. At least that is what the Bible says. If the Bible says it, you can take it to the bank, for it shall surely come to pass!!

Ephesians 3:20a states

"Now to Him who is able to do exceedingly, abundantly above all that we ask or think, according to the power that works in us,"

Remember the story of Charlie? Well, it was my obedience that caused his blessing. I don't boast in this, I am only stating it as an example for this portion of the book. We can see in this example that <u>obedience wins</u>!!

I have another personal example I 'd like to share with you. It started like this ...

I was a new believer in Christ. The church platform was staged for a live telecast of a telethon to raise money for Christian television. I was in the lobby, looking through the windows of the sanctuary doors and wishing I could go inside. Since I was pretty new, I didn't know if it was okay to enter or not. I stood there and realized it would be fine to go in, after all, there were several people in there already and there was going to be live worship for several hours.

The telethon had begun and my heart began to be happy as I entered into the sanctuary. I sat down about half way into the sanctuary so I could see everything. I had only been sitting a moment when the Pastor, my Pastor at the time, said, "I believe ten people are going to give $1000 before this telecast is over." (Yes, this was a long time ago. $10,000 sure wouldn't do much these days. This was over 30 years ago) I sat there full of awe and anticipation. I have to be honest, I was a telethon junkie!! I used to stay up all night to watch the Jerry Lewis Labor Day telethons, and yes, even as a child, I usually gave something.

I was sitting there, enjoying the ministers, when all of a sudden, the Lord said, "You are going to be one of those to give $1000." I literally looked around me to see who was speaking. This was the first time I had audibly heard the voice of Jesus. At that moment, I did not know where the voice had come from. It was so clear, so personal. It took me just a few more times to recognize it was my precious

Savior's voice. (Kind of reminds me of when the Lord was speaking to Samuel and Samuel kept going to Eli to see what he wanted, when in fact it was the Lord Himself Who was speaking to Samuel. *See 1 Samuel 3

As I continued to sit in the sanctuary, listening to the various Christian artists, Pastor Foreman repeated, "Ten of you will give $1000. Just as quickly, the Lord spoke to me again, "You are going to be one of the ten to give $1000." Okay, NOW I was sure it was the Lord. Our conversation went something like this.

LORD: You are going to be one of the ten to give $1000

me: I am going to give $1000 to Christian television? (CLARIFYING)

LORD: You are going to give $1000 to Christian television

me: But God, I have a huge hospital bill (ARGUING)

LORD: You are going to be one of the ten to give $1000

me: BUT GOD, I was going to give my parents new carpet for Christmas (NOT LISTENING)

LORD: I will get your parents new carpet for Christmas.

(LISTENING!!) me: WHAT?

LORD: I will get your parents new carpeting for Christmas. YOU are going to give $1000.

me: YOU ARE GOING TO GET MY PARENTS NEW CARPETING FOR CHRISTMAS?

LORD: I am going to get your parents new carpeting for Christmas. You are going to give $1000

me: OKAY. (SMILING)

[I had this entire conversation out loud and as we say at Soul Harvest..."in HD, 3D, living color."]

I stood up, left my seat, went up front to the table where the telethon operators were working and submitted my pledge for $1000 toward Christian television. Then, I proceeded out the lobby exit to peek through the window and hear Pastor Foreman announce, the last of the ten people had pledged, as they were just about to close out the telethon for the night. I didn't realize how lengthy a conversation the Lord had with me, but then, I think it was because He was allowing me to be ministered to through the worship and the Word going forth in between our conversation. After all, I was baby Christian. I did send in my monthly gift toward Christian television that year and for many years to come.

Do you want to know about His end of the deal? Of course, God did give my parents new carpeting for Christmas!! As a matter of fact, HE gave them a brand new home, brand new appliances, brand new everything!! He did much more than give us the carpet, He taught me that His Word is as good as DONE. I began to easily and quickly recognize the voice of God after that. I am blessed to say, He has spoken to me just as clearly and as personally many, many times since. I wish I could say I have always answered as quickly and easily.

We see in this example how obedience wins!! When I was obedient to the Word of God, I was blessed with the finances to give $1000 toward Christian television, my parents were blessed with a brand new home, which included their brand new carpet (just as the Lord had promised) and many friends and family were blessed to hear the story of how faithful God was to provide us with this beautiful new home just as He had promised me.

[By the way, my hospital bill was paid in full with no lack in payments while still meeting the commitment I had made to Christian television. Glory to God]

So, now let's look at how disobedience causes us to lose.

Perhaps we should look at the Prophet Jonah as an example of "disobedience." In Jonah the first chapter the Lord tells Jonah to go to the city of Nineveh and warn the people that their wickedness has come up before Him. Jonah does not go to the city to warn the people. Jonah disobeys God, gets on a ship and then ends up in the mouth and the belly of a whale. If Jonah does not get the warning to the people, they will not even have the opportunity to repent. (Disobedience loses)

Jonah 1:1-3 (NKJV)

Jonah's Disobedience

1 Now the word of the Lord came to Jonah the son of Amittai, saying, ² "Arise, go to Nineveh, that great city, and cry out against it; for their wickedness has come up before Me." ³ But Jonah arose to flee to Tarshish from the presence of the Lord. He went down to Joppa, and found a ship going to Tarshish; so he paid the fare, and went down into it, to go with them to Tarshish from the presence of the Lord.

Jonah thought he could run from his assignment.

[Interestingly, God never desired to bring harm or judgment to Nineveh. On the contrary, He simply wanted them to change their ways (repent) and this was not going to happen if Jonah was disobedient to warn them.]

You see, I lose, and you lose when we are disobedient to God. Contrarily, when we are obedient, you win, and I win. It works just the same for both of us. This happens because we are connected. We are all part of the same body. THE BODY OF CHRIST.

The Bible says it this way …

Romans 12:4-5

"For as we have many members in one body, but all the members do not have the same function, ⁵ so we, being

many, are one body in Christ, and individually members of one another."

I look at it this way, one of us, most likely you, is the heart, another is the arm or leg, while I am perhaps the toe or toenail. I don't say that in some self loathing way, God forbid. I mention a part of the foot because I desire to be close to Him, the Foundation; I also would like to think I am steady enough for other members to rely upon and lean upon, when necessary.

With or without our realization, we all effect one another. What we say and do, what we believe or doubt, what we pray and fail to pray, matters. We should matter to one another. We need one another. As a body, we won't last without one another. Maybe you've met people, Christians, who think what they do and say doesn't really matter, or worse, they think it doesn't affect anyone else. I can tell you this, it does matter and I will show you in just a moment how the actions of one can and do make a difference.

"Being an armor bearer isn't always comfortable, it doesn't always feel good. Being an armor bearer doesn't mean your friends or family, IT MEANS, you're faithful. It means you care. It means you're there! Being an armor bearer means you're loyal, dependable, reliable, trustworthy, loving and jealous for the honor that is due the subject of interest."

Patty Handly

The Butterfly Effect

I liken this to the Butterfly Effect. The theory is simple, yet challenging. The theory states that some butterfly a million miles away flutters her wings and her actions change the entire universe!! Okay, (maybe) that's exaggerating a bit. Maybe it's more like, a butterfly a million miles away flutters her wings and with that little action, that seemingly insignificant friction, she causes a tidal wave or an earthquake in a completely different part of the world.

The whole idea or concept is based upon the theory of chaos. It is a belief that it is completely possible to affect not only your own atmosphere, but the atmosphere of others hundreds and thousands of miles away, who do not even know your name, or your position. (that's my take on the Butterfly Effect; it is not gospel)

If I think about this "Chaos Theory," long enough, I would consider how each of our pasts, in part, effects our futures. Kind of like the 'self professed prophesy' or how the "pain of an event" effects us internally and perhaps manifests itself externally years later. While I believe we do not have to allow our past to define us, I do believe, in part, it does have an influence on who we become. (at least until Jesus fixes us)

[You can find more information about the Butterfly Effect from Wikipedia, the free encyclopedia online or at your local, almost forgotten, public library.]

The Actions of One

Throughout Scripture, we see how the actions of one often changed the course of History. We can read how the actions of "one righteous" changed the heart and the decisions of the Lord. There are many named in the Bible, who put the needs of others ahead of their own. They challenged God by having faith to stand in the gap for another. They took chances and trusted their relationship with God enough to plead the case of another.

These people, ordinary people, like you and like me, thought they may be able to make a difference, or at least they were willing to step out in faith and try. We can call them armor bearers as well. They truly were God's armor bearers in that, we know the Lord is *"not willing that any should perish but that all should come to repentance."* 2 Peter 3:9, (NKJV)

THE ACTIONS OF DAVID

Let's start with the shepherd boy, David. We read about David and his "actions" in the book of 1 Samuel. We see the faith of David as he listened to the Philistine giant antagonize the Israelites. While all the warriors were doing a whole lot of NOTHING, young David was provoked to action as he began to question why nothing was being done to this uncircumcised enemy of the Lord. David alone stood up and said he would fight this giant.

Although, we read that David appeared to be in this situation because his Father sent him to go and bring food to his brothers, we know that this was in fact a true assignment of God to work His purposes through His servant David. Even in this example we see how David's obedience to his earthly Father set him up for His heavenly appointment with destiny.

1 Samuel 17:17-32

17 And Jesse said to David his son, Take for your brothers an ephah of this parched grain and these ten loaves and carry them quickly to your brothers at the camp.

18 Also take these ten cheeses to the commander of their thousand. See how your brothers fare and bring some token from them.

19 Now Saul and the brothers and all the men of Israel were in the Valley of Elah, fighting with the Philistines.

20 So David rose up early next morning, left the sheep with a keeper, took the provisions, and went, as Jesse had commanded him. And he came to the encampment as the host going forth to the battleground shouted the battle cry.

21 And Israel and the Philistines put the battle in array, army against army.

²² David left his packages in the care of the baggage keeper and ran into the ranks and came and greeted his brothers.

²³ As they talked, behold, Goliath, the champion, the Philistine of Gath, came forth from the Philistine ranks and spoke the same words as before, and David heard him.

²⁴ And all the men of Israel, when they saw the man, fled from him, terrified.

²⁵ And the Israelites said, Have you seen this man who has come out? Surely he has come out to defy Israel; and the man who kills him the king will enrich with great riches, and will give him his daughter and make his father's house free [from taxes and service] in Israel.

²⁶ And David said to the men standing by him, What shall be done for the man who kills this Philistine and takes away the reproach from Israel? For who is this uncircumcised Philistine that he should defy the armies of the living God?

²⁷ And the [men] told him, Thus shall it be done for the man who kills him.

²⁸ Now Eliab his eldest brother heard what he said to the men; and Eliab's anger was kindled against David and he said, Why did you come here? With whom have you left those few sheep in the wilderness? I know your presumption and evilness of heart; for you came down that you might see the battle.

²⁹ And David said, What have I done now? Was it not a harmless question?

³⁰ And David turned away from Eliab to another and he asked the same question, and again the men gave him the same answer.

³¹ When David's words were heard, they were repeated to Saul, and he sent for him.

³² David said to Saul, Let no man's heart fail because of this Philistine; your servant will go out and fight with him.

Unlike the accusations of his brothers, David did not do this boastfully or in his own power, rather he knew THE LORD would bring about the victory. When the King heard that David was willing to face the Philistine giant he sent for him. David told the King, "I will fight!" (My Pastor teaches "I will" is the strongest assertion in the English language)

Without the Kings armor, David left the King, picked up 5 stones and swung away, aiming and hitting his target Goliath smack dab in the forehead, knocking him down and out with that very first stone. I've included the rest of the story so you can read it as well. I love that David stood up for the Lord.

1 Samuel 17:33-58

³³ And Saul said to David, You are not able to go to fight against this Philistine. You are only an adolescent, and he has been a warrior from his youth.

34 *And David said to Saul, Your servant kept his father's sheep. And when there came a lion or again a bear and took a lamb out of the flock,*

35 *I went out after it and smote it and delivered the lamb out of its mouth; and when it arose against me, I caught it by its beard and smote it and killed it.*

36 *Your servant killed both the lion and the bear; and this uncircumcised Philistine shall be like one of them, for he has defied the armies of the living God!*

37 *David said, The Lord Who delivered me out of the paw of the lion and out of the paw of the bear, He will deliver me out of the hand of this Philistine. And Saul said to David, Go, and the Lord be with you!*

38 *Then Saul clothed David with his armor; he put a bronze helmet on his head and clothed him with a coat of mail.*

39 *And David girded his sword over his armor. Then he tried to go, but could not, for he was not used to it. And David said to Saul, I cannot go with these, for I am not used to them. And David took them off.*

40 *Then he took his staff in his hand and chose five smooth stones out of the brook and put them in his shepherd's [lunch] bag [a whole kid's skin slung from his shoulder], in his pouch, and his sling was in his hand, and he drew near the Philistine.*

⁴¹ The Philistine came on and drew near to David, the man who bore the shield going before him.

⁴² And when the Philistine looked around and saw David, he scorned and despised him, for he was but an adolescent, with a healthy reddish color and a fair face.

⁴³ And the Philistine said to David, Am I a dog, that you should come to me with sticks? And the Philistine cursed David by his gods.

⁴⁴ The Philistine said to David, Come to me, and I will give your flesh to the birds of the air and the beasts of the field.

⁴⁵ Then said David to the Philistine, You come to me with a sword, a spear, and a javelin, but I come to you in the name of the Lord of hosts, the God of the ranks of Israel, Whom you have defied.

⁴⁶ This day the Lord will deliver you into my hand, and I will smite you and cut off your head. And I will give the corpses of the army of the Philistines this day to the birds of the air and the wild beasts of the earth, that all the earth may know that there is a God in Israel.

⁴⁷ And all this assembly shall know that the Lord saves not with sword and spear; for the battle is the Lord's, and He will give you into our hands.

⁴⁸ When the Philistine came forward to meet David, David ran quickly toward the battle line to meet the Philistine.

49 David put his hand into his bag and took out a stone and slung it, and it struck the Philistine, sinking into his forehead, and he fell on his face to the earth.

50 So David prevailed over the Philistine with a sling and with a stone, and struck down the Philistine and slew him. But no sword was in David's hand.

51 So he ran and stood over the Philistine, took his sword and drew it out of its sheath, and killed him, and cut off his head with it. When the Philistines saw that their mighty champion was dead, they fled.

52 And the men of Israel and Judah rose with a shout and pursued the Philistines as far as Gath and the gates of Ekron. So the wounded Philistines fell along the way from Shaaraim as far as Gath and Ekron.

53 The Israelites returned from their pursuit of the Philistines and plundered their tents.

54 David took the head of the Philistine and brought it to Jerusalem, but he put his armor in his tent.

55 When Saul saw David go out against the Philistine, he said to Abner, the captain of the host, Abner, whose son is this youth? And Abner said, As your soul lives, O king, I cannot tell.

56 And the king said, Inquire whose son the stripling is.

⁵⁷ When David returned from killing Goliath the Philistine, Abner brought him before Saul with the head of the Philistine in his hand.

⁵⁸ And Saul said to him, Whose son are you, young man? And David answered, I am the son of your servant Jesse of Bethlehem.

David did not allow himself to do nothing when His God was being defiled with the words of the enemy. Instead, he rose up and he took action and the battle with the Philistines was won. His action caused the Philistine army to run in retreat after their leader had fallen at the hand of David.

I find it interesting that the shepherd boy was not interested in fame or glory or even of recognition or position. Yet, his actions captured the attention and admiration of the King. David was inquired of, and sought out, and given a place of honor and position. The Bible says, (1 Samuel 18:2) *"Saul took him that day (into his home) and he would not let him go home to his Father's house anymore."* (NKJV) David entered into his destiny on THIS DAY OF ACTION.

THE ACTIONS OF ABRAHAM

When the Lord was grieved with the wickedness of man's sin in Sodom and Gomorrah, He wanted to destroy the cities with all of their inhabitants. We know Abraham stood in the gap and pleaded to the Lord not to destroy His people, "What if there be 50 righteous? 40? 30? 10? He would not let up, he knew the Lord's heart was NOT to destroy, but to pour out His love and favor upon His creation. Abraham knew he could speak to the Lord and stand in the gap, without fear. Abraham knew the Lord would listen to him. It was his relationship with God the Father that allowed him to take action on behalf of any that may be righteous, especially his family who dwelt in the land.

Genesis 18:18-33 Amplified Bible (AMP)

23 And Abraham came close and said, Will You destroy the righteous (those upright and in right standing with God) together with the wicked?

24 Suppose there are in the city fifty righteous; will You destroy the place and not spare it for [the sake of] the fifty righteous in it?

25 Far be it from You to do such a thing—to slay the righteous with the wicked, so that the righteous fare as do the wicked! Far be it from You! Shall not the Judge of all the earth execute judgment and do righteously?

26 And the Lord said, If I find in the city of Sodom fifty righteous (upright and in right standing with God), I will spare the whole place for their sake.

27 Abraham answered, Behold now, I who am but dust and ashes have taken upon myself to speak to the Lord.

28 If five of the fifty righteous should be lacking—will You destroy the whole city for lack of five? He said, If I find forty-five, I will not destroy it.

²⁹ And [Abraham] spoke to Him yet again, and said, Suppose [only] forty shall be found there. And He said, I will not do it for forty's sake.

³⁰ Then [Abraham] said to Him, Oh, let not the Lord be angry, and I will speak [again]. Suppose [only] thirty shall be found there. And He answered, I will not do it if I find thirty there.

³¹ And [Abraham] said, Behold now, I have taken upon myself to speak [again] to the Lord. Suppose [only] twenty shall be found there. And [the Lord] replied, I will not destroy it for twenty's sake.

³² And he said, Oh, let not the Lord be angry, and I will speak again only this once. Suppose ten [righteous people] shall be found there. And [the Lord] said, I will not destroy it for ten's sake.

³³ And the Lord went His way when He had finished speaking with Abraham, and Abraham returned to his place.

Unlike the story we read about David, this story is sad, in that, although Moses gave it his best shot, Sodom and Gomorrah were not spared, but in fact destroyed since there were not ten righteous men to be found. As we just read, the Lord said, "I will not destroy it for ten's sake." *Genesis 18:32

Although we know there were not 10 righteous men found, God still provided a way of escape for Lot and his family before the destruction of Sodom and Gomorrah. I believe Lot and his family were spared only because of the prayers and pleading of Abraham, not because of their righteousness. Abraham's attempt to save all the souls in the two cities did fail, but his prayers were not in vain, as I am sure Lot and his family would testify. No prayer we ever pray is without result. If we are praying according to the heart of God, we will always have an answer. The Lord always hears the prayers of man. He never ignores anyone who is truly seeking Him.

THE ACTIONS OF JONAH (take two)

I believe the Old Testament Prophets were God's armor bearers as well. They went where the Lord told them to go and they spoke what God said speak, even when it was uncomfortable to them. They did this because they loved God and they trusted Him to do whatsoever He said. Even though the message was oftentimes disheartening, they still obeyed God. That is what TRUE armor bearers do, they follow instructions and they serve with the utmost obedience that stems from a root of love.

Sure, Jonah initially disobeyed the Lord's command and ended up in the belly of a whale, but God is a God of second chances and He always desires His people be saved. Jonah was given a second opportunity to go to Nineveh to give the Word of the Lord to repent and he took it. As we read earlier, he took that chance and this time his actions were actions of obedience as he delivered the Word and the people repented. Our actions will always bring 'results.'

Here are just of few of some of the "actions" we read about in Scripture. I believe each of these men to be an armor bearer of the Lord God.

Abraham "<u>believed</u>" God.

Moses "<u>sought</u>" God.

David "<u>defended</u>" God.

Jacob "<u>wrestled</u>" with God.

Joseph "<u>obeyed</u>" God.

[To be fair to the faithful Women, here are a few of my favorite female armor bearers.]

Ruth, armor bearer to Naomi

Esther, armor bearer to the nation of Israel

Mary, (the one who gave birth to Jesus) armor bearer to humanity.

[Now I'd like to mention the most important, most influential armor bearer of all.]

Jesus, <u>TRUSTED (AND TRUSTS)</u> GOD. ***Because of His trust in God the Father, you and I have the opportunity to have eternal life, due to His sacrifice on the cross. He paid the price for your sin, and for my sin. It is finished. Once, and for all, it is finished.

Are you getting the picture? We are all called to be armor bearers. We are all created to serve one another and as we serve others, we are serving God Himself.

I want to be among those whose obedience impacts the world. I want to be one who has a butterfly effect. NO!! I WANT TO HAVE A TSUMANI EFFECT ON THIS WORLD!! (And nobody needs to know my name) Come on somebody! How many of you even remember the names of those hurricanes anyway. It's not the name that we remember, it's the aftermath we remember, isn't it?

"Being an armor bearer isn't always comfortable, it doesn't always feel good. Being an armor bearer doesn't mean your friends or family, IT MEANS, you're faithful. It means you care. It means you're there! Being an armor bearer means you're loyal, dependable, reliable, trustworthy, loving and jealous for the honor that is due the subject of interest."

Patty Handly

Excuses, Excuses, Excuses!

You may be asking yourself, as I have in my lifetime, "Who am I that God would use me or ask anything of me?" What can I do that could possibly make a difference in the life of, well, anyone? Or, you may simply be one who makes excuses when you do hear the Lord calling upon you. Or, perhaps, it is your Pastor, or your boss, or even, your brother, asking something of you. Here are just a few excuses we read about in the Bible from some men in the Bible.

"I HAVE RESPONSIBILITIES I NEED TO TAKE CARE OF **FIRST!**"

Luke 9:59-60 (AMP)

⁵⁹ And He said to another, Become My disciple, side with My party, and accompany Me! But he replied, Lord, permit me first to go and bury (await the death of) my father.

⁶⁰ But Jesus said to him, Allow the dead to bury their own dead; but as for you, go and publish abroad throughout all regions the kingdom of God.

"I HAVE OTHER THINGS I NEED TO HANDLE **FIRST!**"

Luke 9:61 (AMP)

⁶¹ Another also said, I will follow You, Lord, and become Your disciple and side with Your party; but let me first say good-bye to those at my home.

"I AM POOR, I AM NOTHING COMPARED TO OTHERS" (Gideon)

Judges 6:15The Message (MSG)

¹⁵ Gideon said to him, "Me, my master? How and with what could I ever save Israel? Look at me. My clan's the weakest in Manasseh and I'm the runt of the litter."

"I AM TOO YOUNG" (Jeremiah)

Jeremiah 1:6

⁶ Then said I, Ah, Lord God! Behold, I cannot speak, for I am only a youth.

Moses is my favorite example. He doesn't have just one excuse, he has a full list. How many of us would be honest enough to say we have had more than one excuse for not moving when God has asked us, or not doing what God has called us to do? Here is the list of some of the excuses our dear Moses presented to the Lord. Now keep in mind, Moses had a beautiful relationship with the Almighty God of eternity. In fact, the Lord refers to Moses as his friend in Genesis 18:17 (AMP)

"I AM NOT QUALIFIED" (Exodus 3:11)

"I DON'T KNOW ENOUGH" (Exodus 3:13)

"I DON'T BELIEVE I CAN" (Exodus 4:1)

"NO ONE WILL LISTEN TO ME" (Exodus 4:1)

"THIS IS NOT MY CALLING" (Exodus 4:10)

"I CANNOT SPEAK" (Exodus 4:10)

"I AM NOT ELOQUENT" (Exodus 4:10)

"I AM SLOW OF SPEECH!! " (Exodus 4:10)

"I DO NOT WANT THIS TO BE MY CALLING, SEND SOMEONE ELSE" (Exodus 4:13)

As I read and write these scriptures, and excuses, I cannot help but think about the other side of the coin. I think about one of one of my favorite writers, the Apostle Paul, who never made excuses to fail or to quit or to not start. Paul always gave us reasons to never make excuses. He was excuseless..

Romans 8:37 New King James Version (NKJV)

37 Yet in all these things we are more than conquerors through Him who loved us.

Philippians 4:13 New King James Version (NKJV)

13 I can do all things through Christ who strengthens me.

[My first Pastor, Kenny Foreman called Philippians 4:13 our "ten finger prayer." It was powerful to think I could call this to mind by just looking at my fingers and declaring this Scripture as MY TRUTH. I just realized this was the first declaration I ever made as a Christian. (not a bad one at that) Amen]

Dear friend, the Bible teaches us that *"death and life are in the power of the tongue"* (Proverbs 18:21) That means, we cannot afford to make excuses or rely upon excuses to prevent us from God's purposes. We must determine in our hearts to speak life, speak truth and make no more excuses.

Single Minded, Stable and Secure

Armor bearers must be single minded, stable and secure. In order to be successful as an armor bearer, we must understand the importance of "mindfulness." We must be mindful, (attentive, aware and careful of) single mindedness.

I love when I am free to run with the vision of my Pastor. I love when I know my heart is right and my motives are right and my heart is single-minded. When I am free to run with the vision of my Pastor and I recognize I am submitted to God and to His will, I am absolutely in my element. I am home. It is here, in this place, that I am happy and content, knowing I am serving God, my Pastor and my church with the purity and integrity that is necessary to accomplish His purposes. When I am single minded, I am always in a state of peace and absolute JOY!!

[That my friend is what being an armor bearer is all about, being single minded]

When I am unfocused, or half focused, I cannot do the will of my Father. If I am only serving with half my heart, half my effort and half my energy, then, I am failing. Remember, if I fail, you fail. If I lose, you lose. We cannot afford to fail, the Lord is counting on us. He is trusting us to pick up the baton and run this race.

I think back to the upper room, when the followers of Christ were all in "one mind and one accord," the Holy Spirit came to them in power and they were all filled with the Holy Ghost. They were all filled with the person and the power of the Holy Spirit. We, as believers are also filled with the presence and the power of the Holy Spirit.

Acts 2:2-4 New King James Version (NKJV)

2 When the Day of Pentecost had fully come, they were all with one accord in one place. ² And suddenly there came a sound from heaven, as of a rushing mighty wind, and it filled the whole house where they were sitting. ³ Then there appeared to them divided tongues, as of fire, and one sat upon each of them. ⁴ And they were all filled with the Holy Spirit and began to speak with other tongues, as the Spirit gave them utterance.

When I think about being in one mind and one accord, I also think about the people who began to build the tower of Babel. This story has always blown my mind, I mean truly, it is unfathomable that it could even be true. Let's read it together …

Genesis 11: 1-9 King James Version (KJV)

1And the whole earth was of one language, and of one speech.

²And it came to pass, as they journeyed from the east, that they found a plain in the land of Shinar; and they dwelt there.

³And they said one to another, Go to, let us make brick, and burn them thoroughly. And they had brick for stone, and slime had they for morter.

⁴And they said, Go to, let us build us a city and a tower, whose top may reach unto heaven; and let us make us a name, lest we be scattered abroad upon the face of the whole earth.

⁵And the Lord came down to see the city and the tower, which the children of men builded.

⁶And the Lord said, Behold, the people is one, and they have all one language; and this they begin to do: and now nothing will be restrained from them, which they have imagined to do.

⁷Go to, let us go down, and there confound their language, that they may not understand one another's speech.

⁸So the Lord scattered them abroad from thence upon the face of all the earth: and they left off to build the city.

⁹Therefore is the name of it called Babel; because the Lord did there confound the language of all the earth: and from thence did the Lord scatter them abroad upon the face of all the earth.

Are you kidding me? Is it truly possible to be in such agreement and such unity that a tower could be built that would touch heaven? Is it just as possible that when we are in agreement and in unity with THE WORD, (JESUS), that we could say to this mountain, be thou cast down, and it would crumble before our feet? Yes. Yes, I say Yes.

John 14:12-14 (KJV)

"If you will believe in your heart (and not doubt), you shall have whatsoever you ask, in my name, that the Father may be glorified in the Son."

Is this the Word of God or isn't it? Let's read that again.

John 14:12-14 King James Version (KJV)

[12] Verily, verily, I say unto you, He that believeth on me, the works that I do shall he do also; and greater works than these shall he do; because I go unto my Father.

[13] And whatsoever ye shall ask in my name, that will I do, that the Father may be glorified in the Son.

[14] If ye shall ask any thing in my name, I will do it.

I pray one day we will begin to have a single minded focus with a "no doubt" conviction in our spirit, so we can never be accused or guilty of being double minded.

Double Minded, Double Blinded

The Word of God says, *"A double minded man is unstable in all of his ways"* (James 1:8)

The Lord cannot accomplish what He desires to accomplish through a half yielded vessel. I must, and you must, be wholly convinced of God's desire to use us as His armor bearers and then, we must be willing to be yielded, teachable and unselfish in all areas of our lives. When we decide to do this, He will help us to actually do it. For the record, WE CANNOT do this without His help.

I will be the example for this section of the book.

If I am thinking about other things, having my focus divided, I cannot be whole hearted. I MUST NOT be thinking about 'my future,' rather, I must be thinking about, "Who holds my future." My focus and my attention must be on 'the NOW,' and not on the tomorrow, or the day after tomorrow.

Believe me when I tell you, I have been tested in that area on many occasions. I cannot be worried, sidetracked, hesitant or halted. I must be on task, on time and on target. The late Rev. Ira Chalk taught this to his daughter, my Pastor, and she taught this to me. I am doing my best to be to be on task, on time and on target.

As a single woman, who desires to be married, I have had to consciously place my husband on the altar and ask the Lord to take the desire to be married away, until at least it is "time" to be concerned about this. Many well meaning friends have told me to pray and believe God for my husband if it is truly a desire of my heart. Others have told me to make a list and tell God exactly the kind of man I really want. They've mentioned describing his features, what I am attracted to in a man, what color hair, how tall, how short. "Be specific." While I know each one of these precious friends has had the best intentions for me, I have never believed this was something I should do, or even needed to do. After all, I know God knows the desires of my heart. He created me. He gave me the desires in my heart. He knows what is best for me and I know "I do not know what is best for me," even when I think I do.

That is why it is important for me to "Submit to God" (period).The Bible says, in Philippians 4:19 (KJV) *" He shall supply all my needs according to His riches in Christ Jesus.* I truly believe God will give me the desires of my heart, in His timing, when HE KNOWS I AM READY and not one second before.

So, I do not pray to be married as much as I used to. I do not pray for God to hurry and send him because I am lonely. Rather, I pray God will replace my loneliness with Himself and that my joy will be made full in Him. If I can simply surrender this desire (and all others) to God, I will not be a double minded person who is unstable in all of my ways. I never want to be that person, (anymore).

I pray to be a faithful armor bearer each day. I pray that my will is submitted to the will of the Father and that my actions (all of my actions) are pleasing to the Him. I oftentimes ask, "What is the one thing I can do that will bless someone this day?" I am always so happy when the Lord shows me and I obey Him. It is always a blessing for me when I know I have been a blessing to another.

"Being an armor bearer isn't always comfortable, it doesn't always feel good. Being an armor bearer doesn't mean your friends or family, IT MEANS, you're faithful. It means you care. It means you're there! Being an armor bearer means you're loyal, dependable, reliable, trustworthy, loving and jealous for the honor that is due the subject of interest."

Patty Handly

Becoming an Armor Bearer

I am my Pastor's armor bearer. I should say, "I am one of many of my Pastor's armor bearers," for there is never only one. Jesus had twelve. (Interestingly, one of His armor bearers betrayed Him, which was no surprise to Him. He chose him in spite of knowing he would be betrayed by this chosen disciple.) I hope to study this matter more diligently in the future.

When I say, "I am my Pastor's armor bearer," I think about Elijah, who said, *"I am the only prophet who remains."* (2 Kings 18:22)

Elijah was not the only prophet who remained, and I am not the only armor bearer that serves my Pastor. Truthfully, I am not even officially an armor bearer, but, I know God called me to be my Pastor's armor bearer, so with or without a title, with or without "the office," I am an armor bearer. This is not anything I brag about, but it is rather, a truly reverent (humbling) position. I'm about to explain why …

As an armor bearer, I have the awesome privilege, as those who've gone before me, to honor and serve my Pastor and the congregation "as unto the Lord." I say "awesome" because of the magnitude of responsibility of the armor bearer, not because it is ALWAYS "exciting and full of awe, " quite the contrary.

As my dear friend, Pastor Henry Killings shared with his congregation once, "An armor bearer sees the leader, the Pastor, *the subject of interest,* in all of his or her humanity. He sees them often in their raw humanness, and that is not always a pretty sight." (Italics added)

Becoming an armor bearer is a process, it is not a position to be taken lightly, or carefree. God forbid. I believe the Lord allows the armor bearer to see the humanity of the Pastor in order that he may pray more diligently for him/ her. I also believe this revealing of humanity prevents the armor bearer from placing his subject of interest on a pedestal or from making him a god. It is important that we recognize "no one is perfect and we all deserve to have grace extended." Amen.

As I have alluded previously, the responsibilities of the armor bearer are to support, encourage, serve, honor, and pray for the Pastor. But, other than prayer, it is most important, to lay down his plans and his 'future' PLANS FOR HIMSELF, in order to keep focused on the plans and vision of the Pastor. When we are able to run with the vision of our Pastors, abandoning our own vision, we are free to serve with a grateful heart and a unwavering confidence in God.

While it is important to know and understand what an armor bearer is to do, it is just as important to know and understand what an armor bearer should NEVER DO. For example, armor bearers should not struggle with FLESH FLASHES or hidden agendas (hidden motives, hidden goals). We have to be people of integrity and loyal to a fault. We must be trustworthy, unselfish, non-threatening and UNTHREATENED. This is not an option. For we shall not be a blessing or bring honor to the Lord, if we are lacking in these areas.

I love how my Pastor always teaches that those of us who are older should desire for our ceiling to be the younger's floor. That is to say, we need to celebrate when those younger than us begin to accomplish more than we ever did. I struggled with this in the beginning of my journey, but thanks be to God, I know understand and whole heartedly believe this and desire this.

Remember in the introduction I mentioned I wanted to help you to not make the same mistakes I have made? Well, I have made enough for many of us. I have had flesh flashes and been insensitive to the needs of others. I have rushed by someone without acknowledging them, perhaps 'on my way to do something.' Perhaps I have hurt someone without cause, without my knowledge due to my own business. But, I am thankful for the correction I have received in times of error and ignorance. Yes, if we are to serve anyone, we must make ourselves available for correction and reproof. That is not always easy and never is it fun, but beloved friend, it is so worth it. I love correction and I love growing from that correction. I would not be the person I am today, had it not been for all the love given me, through the gift of correction.

Proverbs 3:12Amplified Bible (AMP)

12 For whom the Lord loves He corrects, even as a father corrects the son in whom he delights.

I love my Pastor, and I am forever thankful that she loves me enough to teach, train, equip and correct me. I love that, just as a parent takes the time to correct a child, my Pastor loves me and her entire congregation enough to correct us and to teach us the whole truth of the Word, not just the parts that feel good! I honor her in this. She does this "intentionally" in order to bring Jesus the reward of His suffering (souls). I truly believe that God is well pleased with all Pastors who preach the true Gospel, the whole Gospel, the truth and nothing but the truth, so help us God. I honor all Pastors who remain shut in their closets, praying, preparing, seeking God for a true Word to preach to His church, each and every service. Thank you all for your integrity in serving HIM. God bless you each and everyone.

Many are Called

We, the Body of Christ, are all called to be <u>ministers and servants</u>. I believe those words are synonymous with "armor bearers." I believe all Christians are called to be God's faithful armor bearers. I believe each member of the congregation is meant to be an armor bearer to the Pastor God has placed over him. Yes, I said, "placed, over" him.

A true Pastor, called of God, is placed in a position of AUTHORITY over a congregation. He or she is responsible for the flock, not the clock. (That my friend, is another book) It is the assignment of the Lord for the Pastor to lead the flock by training and equipping them for the work of the ministry. Now, I understand the work of the ministry is to go out into the field and bring in the harvest, but I also believe, in the process, the armor bearer is developed in character and maturity.

As responsible members of a congregation, and faithful servants of the Lord Jesus Christ, I believe we are to follow the teaching of Scripture and serve our Pastors, and one another, as unto God.

The Bible says, in Deuteronomy 6:5 (KJV)

"⁵And thou shalt love the Lord thy God with all thine heart, and with all thy soul, and with all thy might."

That is exactly what it means to serve.

Think about it for just a second. Don't you love to serve, and bless your loved ones? Don't you love blessing them with their favorite things and pouring out upon them the things that make them the most happy? Don't you love to take care of them and do things that will perhaps lift their burdens or take away some of their trouble? I do. I absolutely love it. I love waking up in the morning and asking the Lord how I can bless someone each day.

I love knowing, and believing that my desire to bless does not end with just my 'loved ones.' I love blessing the "stranger" because I believe God Himself is found in the heart of the stranger. I love thinking about James, the man I see over by the McDonalds, who I try to bless with a cold beverage or a hamburger when I am able. I love that I look for the regulars to share part of my breakfast with. If I order the largest meal on the menu, I usually put some aside for the person the Lord will lead me to. I love knowing that my King Jesus and my heavenly Father care for the orphans and widows and that They care for me, and provide for all my our needs. I love that They are willing to trust me to carry out Their heart to the multitude. I do, I do, I really do. I love being used as His faithful servant, His faithful armor bearer.

To be perfectly honest, I am MOST HAPPY when I know God has made a way for me to bless "MPP." That is to say, "My Precious Pastor." I say I am most happy because I believe when I am blessing her, and her family I am blessing the nations. I know God has anointed her to be an armor bearer for the nations. She is a vital part of what God is doing right now, in this season. The Lord has raised her up to be a Prophetic voice to this region and to the utter most parts of the earth. She is mighty prayer warrior and a fierce woman of the Word of God. She operates in the full anointing of God and moves when He moves and speaks what He speaks. She is a woman of honor and I believe in the ministry God has called her to. So, if I do the math, when I bless her, I am seeding into an exponential harvest of souls, ministries and leaders, and that is a pretty good deal, if you ask me.

I also love to bless her because she has been a tremendous blessing to me, as a Pastor, a teacher and a friend. I don't take any of this lightly, I have alluded to this already, but for clarity sake I will state it outright; the Lord has spoken very clearly to my heart about how I am to treat Pastor Verna Brown. I don't need a title or a position, I have been given a mandate from God Himself and I will serve and honor my Pastor as long as my precious Lord allows me the privilege. I pray I will never leave her or her family, or this church without the blessing of God, and her blessing. I am wholly committed to giving my all, in the line of duty, as a living sacrifice unto God, for His glory and His honor, as His example of a true armor bearer. I will finish my race, I will complete the task at hand and I will pray daily that I am a faithful and true armor bearer.

I have not placed my Pastor on a pedestal nor do I think she is perfect. I do however believe in her and I will stand with her because I believe what the LORD has spoken to my heart concerning her. I've already stated, no one is perfect and no one should ever hold the place of honor that is meant only for the Lord. But, when God gives you an assignment, He will give you instructions and He will show you how to do the task at hand. He is the one who is leading me in my assignment as my Pastor's armor bearer and He alone do I hold in the HIGHEST PLACE OF HONOR, far, far above the place of honor I hold my Pastor in. (I added this paragraph to clarify the position of honor I hold my Pastor in, for the person who would be concerned, so I do not put a stumbling block before them. I do hope it helps anyone who needed the clarification)

Answering the Call

Yes, we have heard, many are called, but just because we are called, doesn't mean, we always answer! Right? How many of you have called your children into the house at suppertime? Have they always come running in, as soon as they heard the call? If they are anything like I was as a child, it sometimes took more than one call. It sometimes took more than one voice. All I am saying is this ...

The Lord is calling. Is He calling you? Is He calling you to be His armor bearer? Do you attend a local church? Have you 'committed' to a local church? Have you submitted to the headship and the authority of your Pastor? Will you? Remember, "I WILL" is the greatest assertion in the English language. It is an act (action) of the heart and without it, we will not accomplish much.

Is the Lord calling you to be an armor bearer and to serve your Pastor? Are you willing to pray about it? I challenge you to pray about what the Lord would have you do.

"Being an armor bearer isn't always comfortable, it doesn't always feel good. Being an armor bearer doesn't mean your friends or family, IT MEANS, you're faithful. It means you care. It means you're there! Being an armor bearer means you're loyal, dependable, reliable, trustworthy, loving and jealous for the honor that is due the subject of interest."

Patty Handly

Prayer is Not an Option

A long, long time ago, I was sharing with a friend of mine about church membership. I had no idea of the views this person had regarding the matter, so when I learned church membership was not important to my friend, I was upset. As you can imagine, I was shocked and devastated we were having this conversation at all. I mean, after all, this person was a solid Christian believer whom I loved and I was choking on our conversation.

My friend was explaining taking membership was not important. I thought, NOT IMPORTANT? How can we submit to authority, unless we first HAVE PLACED OURSELVES UNDER AUTHORITY? I mean, how can we be a part of a congregation or even call a Pastor, Pastor, unless we have first made covenant with that Pastor? Our conversation was not headed anywhere, so we simply let it go, but it gnawed at me.

When I asked my friend to "pray about it," the response was, "I don't need to pray about it." (Another blow to my heart) You don't need to pray about it? YOU DON'T NEED TO PRAY ABOUT IT? My mind was spinning. I kept thinking,

You don't need to pray about it? OR, you won't pray about it? (There is a huge difference)

Later, in another conversation, my friend clarified, "It isn't a piece of paper that states you're a member to a congregation that makes you a member, it is the commitment in your heart and your actions of service and tithing that make you a member, paper or no paper." So, it wasn't so much this person was against praying about this area, it was just a matter of the heart. I understood what my friend was saying, but I also recognized my friend didn't just 'live with' the partner God had given. My friend has a legal document, a marriage license, (a covenant was made) verified authorization of the unity between this man and this woman in matrimony.

In my first book, "My Story, His Glory," I include a prayer. I do so because in my heart, I truly believe if someone prays this prayer, he will be set free. When I was living in a lifestyle displeasing to God, I always prayed that the Lord would have His way in me and I always prayed He would correct me if I were in error. Needless to say, the Lord did correct me and love me into His perfect will. It happened when I was "fully submitted" to prayer, answering the bidding He had made. He changed my heart in a second, and I have never been the same. I believe wholly in the power of prayer. I don't believe Jesus did anything without prayer. I believe He was always on task, on time, and on target because HE WAS (HE IS) ALWAYS ON PURPOSE.

God is Always "On Purpose"

If I may state the obvious, God is always ON PURPOSE. The Bible teaches us that the Lord created everything, "for a purpose," with intent. Yes, everything God does and everything He created is 'INTENTIONAL.' The earth and the sky provide us with our home and the breath He breathed into us gave us life itself. This breath allows us to live and move and have our being, in HIM. Let's read it in the Word.

Colossians 1:16-17 The Message (MSG)

For everything, absolutely everything, above and below, visible and invisible, rank after rank after rank of angels— everything got started in him and finds its purpose in him. He was there before any of it came into existence and holds it all together right up to this moment.

Revelation 4:11 (KJV) King James Version

[11] Thou art worthy, O Lord, to receive glory and honour and power: for thou hast created all things, and for thy pleasure they are and were created.

Acts 17:24-28 (NKJV) New King James Version

[24] *"God, who made the world and everything in it, since He is Lord of heaven and earth, does not dwell in temples made with hands. [25] Nor is He worshiped with men's hands, as though He needed anything, since He gives to all life, breath, and all things. [26] And He has made from one blood every nation of men to dwell on all the face of the earth, and has determined their pre-appointed times and the boundaries of their dwellings, [27] so that they should seek the Lord, in the hope that they might grope for Him and find Him, though He is not far from each one of us; [28] for in Him we live and move and have our being, as also some of your own poets have said, 'For we are also His offspring.'*

Did you get that? (Acts 17:28b)

[28] 'For we are also His offspring.'

Becoming Adopted

As Christians, we are children of God. That means, we have been adopted by our heavenly Father, as we just read in Acts 17:28, 'we are His offspring!'. We have received His name, and we are no longer orphans! My favorite scriptures on this subject are found in the books of Romans, Galatians, and Ephesians. These are probably my most favorite books in the entire Bible. Although I love Genesis and the Gospels BEST of all because they speak (to me) of the love of God, more than any other books.

Romans 8:15 Amplified Bible (AMP)

¹⁵ For [the Spirit which] you have now received [is] not a spirit of slavery to put you once more in bondage to fear, but you have received the Spirit of adoption [the Spirit producing sonship] in [the bliss of] which we cry, Abba (Father)! Father!

Galatians 4:4-7 (KJV)

⁴ But when the fulness of the time was come, God sent forth his Son, made of a woman, made under the law,

⁵ To redeem them that were under the law, that we might receive the adoption of sons.

⁶ And because ye are sons, God hath sent forth the Spirit of his Son into your hearts, crying, Abba, Father.

⁷ Wherefore thou art no more a servant, but a son; and if a son, then an heir of God through Christ.

Ephesians 1:1-6

³ Blessed be the God and Father of our Lord Jesus Christ, who has blessed us with every spiritual blessing in the heavenly places in Christ, ⁴ just as He chose us in Him before the foundation of the world, that we should be holy and without blame before Him in love, ⁵ having predestined us to adoption as sons by Jesus Christ to Himself, according to the good pleasure of His will, ⁶ to the praise of the glory of His grace, by which He made us accepted in the Beloved.

While I do not profess to be an expert on adoption, (yet), I plan to be. I know there are couples who have a radical calling to adopt, bringing in 10-12 children in their home at one time. There are also those who have traveled great distance, to China and Romania and to the utter most parts of the earth to adopt a child. To date, I have adopted two sons whom I have loved as my own. So, you see, I know what it is to both adopt and be adopted. I received my personal adoption spiritually, while my sons received adoption from me first and then, thankfully from our heavenly Father.

[It is imperative that you and I understand this point; if you or I fail to understand our position as a son of God, we will never be able to truly become faithful armor bearers to our King.]

"Being an armor bearer isn't always comfortable, it doesn't always feel good. Being an armor bearer doesn't mean your friends or family, IT MEANS, you're faithful. It means you care. It means you're there! Being an armor bearer means you're loyal, dependable, reliable, trustworthy, loving and jealous for the honor that is due the subject of interest."

Patty Handly

Extraordinary Love

I cannot possibly write a book about becoming God's faithful armor bearer, without mentioning God's extraordinary love. I mean, after all, without His love, we would have no desire, no design and no example for such a life of servanthood. Through the examples we have in scripture, we are able to know the heart of God and that my friend, is where it all begins.

God is AWESOME! He is amazing!! First, He creates us in His image and likeness. (Genesis 1:26-30). Then, He blesses us with EVERY spiritual blessing. (Philippians 4:19) THEN … in case that wasn't enough to convince us of His love, He does the unthinkable, the unimaginable, He pays a debt we owe and never requires us to pay Him back, EVER. As a matter of fact, we could not repay this debt even if we wanted to, but God already knew that and He came through anyway.

Genesis 1:26-30 Amplified Bible (AMP)

²⁶ God said, Let Us [Father, Son, and Holy Spirit] make mankind in Our image, after Our likeness, and let them have complete authority over the fish of the sea, the birds of the air, the [tame] beasts, and over all of the earth, and over everything that creeps upon the earth.[A]

[27] *So God created man in His own image, in the image and likeness of God He created him; male and female He created them.*[B]

[28] *And God blessed them and said to them, Be fruitful, multiply, and fill the earth, and subdue it [using all its vast resources in the service of God and man]; and have dominion over the fish of the sea, the birds of the air, and over every living creature that moves upon the earth.*

[29] *And God said, See, I have given you every plant yielding seed that is on the face of all the land and every tree with seed in its fruit; you shall have them for food.*

[30] *And to all the animals on the earth and to every bird of the air and to everything that creeps on the ground—to everything in which there is the breath of life—I have given every green plant for food. And it was so.*

Ephesians 1:3 American Standard Version (ASV)

[3] *Blessed be the God and Father of our Lord Jesus Christ, who hath blessed us with every spiritual blessing in the heavenly places in Christ:*

John 3:16-17

¹⁶ For God so loved the world, that he gave his only begotten Son, that whosoever believeth in him should not perish, but have everlasting life.

¹⁷ For God sent not his Son into the world to condemn the world; but that the world through him might be saved.

Jesus pays the penalty of our sin, which is to say, He offers His life, in exchange for ours. He pays our debt, which is "death" and offers us abundant life in exchange.

God the Father, and God the Son, Jesus Christ, have done something that demonstrate more than ordinary love through the gift of salvation, They have demonstrated EXTRAORDINARY LOVE!

"Being an armor bearer isn't always comfortable, it doesn't always feel good. Being an armor bearer doesn't mean your friends or family, IT MEANS, you're faithful. It means you care. It means you're there! Being an armor bearer means you're loyal, dependable, reliable, trustworthy, loving and jealous for the honor that is due the subject of interest."

Patty Handly

Being "Adoptable"

Extraordinary love is what it takes to be an adoptive parent. This is also what it takes to "allow oneself to become adoptable." Yes, it takes a special person to allow someone who is not "the parent" to take the role of the parent. It is a matter of loyalty as well as trust.

Although I could provide care and even minister to my sons, I could in no way be a mom to them without their permission. William and Matty must first have allowed me the privilege to actually be their parent. While this didn't come right away, I now know and believe each, at one time or another came to accept me, truly as his mom. I was blessed with the gift of adopting, and they were blessed with the gift of being adopted.

Did you know a child can be "unadoptable"? Truly, I am not making this up. In this world when there are hundreds of thousands of parentless children, the state or social services can deem a child 'unadoptable'. This is based on the child's behavior, well being, ability to be around others or, for the most part, the safety of others. That sounds absolutely horrifying to me.

I thank God that He does not have any kind of "unadoptable clause in His adoption process." If you want to become adopted, you simply choose to allow Him to be your Dad. You submit to His authority and you allow yourself to be His child,

Every child deserves a chance to be welcomed into a family, a home, and a heart. No matter the situation, no matter the circumstance, we all deserve to have loving parents. If we are without loving parents, we all deserve the opportunity be become adopted.

I will share a secret with you. I believe God is going to do something amazing in my ripe old age. I believe He is going to do miracle after miracle in my life in order to cause me to be an on purpose blessing to many young boys who are in foster care, needing adoption. I am including this in my book because I am taking a giant leap of faith in declaring this awesome future God has in store for me. I believe first, the Lord will provide my beloved husband and together we will bring a hundred boys from the age of 11 through 17 into our home and with time, we will adopt them and bless them with a family, a home and God's love. If there is an 18, 19 or 20 year old who wants a family or a home, God will direct us in that as well.

My sons were not raised with a father in their lives, and they missed out on many wonderful experiences they should have had. It is in my heart to provide an earthly, (yet Godly) father for my son Matty, no matter how old he is when this happens. I pray that boys everywhere would have Godly men in their lives and that they would grow up to be wonderful Godly men, loving husbands and amazing sons.

I believe the Lord will provide my husband and me a beautiful homestead on at least a hundred acres, with a body of water running though it with which my husband will teach our sons to fish. I also believe we will have horses and cattle and should the Lord permit a football field, tennis court, basketball court and lots of animals and unlimited amounts of Christian love. I'm willing to take in as many as we can raise in a healthy environment. We will only will ask for one thing in exchange, "May we have your permission to love you and become your parents?"

"Being an armor bearer isn't always comfortable, it doesn't always feel good. Being an armor bearer doesn't mean your friends or family, IT MEANS, you're faithful. It means you care. It means you're there! Being an armor bearer means you're loyal, dependable, reliable, trustworthy, loving and jealous for the honor that is due the subject of interest."

Patty Handly

Permision Please

As the children of God we must allow the Lord the opportunity to be our Daddy. We must allow Him the opportunity to be our Provider. He so desires to bless us, as we've read previously, with all we have need of. When we give God permission to be our Dad, we will begin to understand what an awesome PRIVILEGE adoption truly is.

When our newly adopted sons grant us permission, they will have the provision, love and inheritance they so deserve as our sons of promise.

I love the subject of adoption because it best describes "belonging to by choice." We all have a choice to receive or reject the adoption God offers us. I LOVE THIS NEXT SCRIPTURE. It really hits the nail on the head.

John 1:12 (NKJV)

12 But as many as received Him, to them He gave the right to become children of God, to those who believe in His name: 13 who were born, not of blood, nor of the will of the flesh, nor of the will of man, but of God.

When we receive adoption, then, only then, do we have the right, the privilege and the honor of being HIS CHILDREN!!

"Being an armor bearer isn't always comfortable, it doesn't always feel good. Being an armor bearer doesn't mean your friends or family, IT MEANS, you're faithful. It means you care. It means you're there! Being an armor bearer means you're loyal, dependable, reliable, trustworthy, loving and jealous for the honor that is due the subject of interest."

Patty Handly

Permission Granted

Adoption is an amazing gift of family. It is a gift to both the parent(s), as well as the child. The very best part of adoption, as I alluded to earlier, is when the child "receives" the adoption, and grants you the permission (acceptance) to become the parent. It's when he allows you to wrap your arms around him and kiss his face and hold him tight. Sure, all of that may not come right away, as I learned with my precious son William, but, in time, it does come and there is nothing sweeter than having the permission to love someone with all the love in your heart. [That is how a mama loves her children and that is how a Daddy loves his children too.]

I loved when I adopted my two sons. The Judge asked the boys how they felt about me adopting them before the adoption process proceeded. At the time, I thought it extra special to include them in the adoption process. NOW, I think it is absolutely NECESSARY to include the child in the adoption process.

I don't know what I would have done if they said, 'NO THANK YOU.' The Judge took his time on this matter, speaking to each one individually and finally having William and Matty each sign a contract showing they agreed to the terms of the adoption. I have pictures I can pull out at any time if I need to, to show it was a joint decision. (big smile)

Becoming the Children of God

I brought all of this up to share this …

Unless we understand Whose we are, we will never truly become who God has called us to be as His sons. I say sons, because we are all the sons of God. As I learned in reading scripture, "the sons" receive the inheritance: the inheritance is sonship. Male or Female, rich or poor, known or unknown, we are the sons of God and as such, we have the inheritance of sonship through adoption.

We must recognize and admit (accept) that we are the children of God. Our inheritance is to be (become) the sons of the Most High. Without exception, we must individually allow the adoption process to lead us into our full inheritance.

"Being an armor bearer isn't always comfortable, it doesn't always feel good. Being an armor bearer doesn't mean your friends or family, IT MEANS, you're faithful. It means you care. It means you're there! Being an armor bearer means you're loyal, dependable, reliable, trustworthy, loving and jealous for the honor that is due the subject of interest."

Patty Handly

The Great Inheritance

If my sons denied or refused to accept they are my children, or if they did not recognize or admit I am their parent, the inheritance I have for them is lost forever. But, if they willingly accept and receive the gift of inheritance, as my children, they will also better be able to receive the Greater Inheritance of sonship that is theirs through faith.

I am thankful to God that my son William was able to accept me as his parent and allow me to minister to him as a Mother before he went home to be with the Lord (at age 19). Most of his life he struggled to be independent. He wanted to be a man so badly, all of his young life, always doing things his way or on his own. But when he truly needed someone, I was so blessed he called upon me, and in the end, he allowed me the privilege to care for him as a Mother. This was the greatest gift he ever gave me, for I knew, he had now accepted me as his mom. I am forever grateful to my Lord for blessing me with this precious gift of love. I love knowing William finally had received his inheritance, the gift of sonship.

I am thankful that my son Matty showed me his love and acceptance one evening, after a Radical Ones Conference.

My home was filled with teenage boys. We had all gone out to eat at the Golden Corral and then returned home with such joy and laughter. We were all sharing and then we began washing each other's feet in my living room, as the Lord's presence was filling my home. Matty had just washed my feet, and then 'out of the blue' said, "Thank you for adopting me and being such a good mom. I love you." It was the first time Matty had ever called me Mom. He doesn't call me that often, but when he does, I know it is intentional and it is always received with a tear in my heart. That night, I knew Matty had received the gift of adoption, I further knew he would receive all the promises God had preordained for him and his children. He would now have his full inheritance, his gift of sonship.

The Bible is full of promises to the generations of God's people. My sons and I, only need to acknowledge our adoption and the promises and inheritance are all ours. I know when my sweet William entered into heaven, he received all the promises he had yet to obtain while upon the earth. He now has his mansion in heaven, and if I know him, he has been having everyone over, every day. He has sought out and found his Grandma Donna, Grandpa Harry, and gone to eat with Mama Donna Wiley and Grandma Chalk. William was always thinking, always deliberate, and always compassionate. I have a feeling deep within my heart that he is asking the Lord to see every single relative he has in heaven and he is making his way to each one's home to introduce himself and offer them a place at his table.

I believe William and Matty have both received the Spirit of Adoption. I believe they have both received the Great Inheritance of Sonship. This belief I hold in my heart, blesses me more than all the treasures in the world.

"Being an armor bearer isn't always comfortable, it doesn't always feel good. Being an armor bearer doesn't mean your friends or family, IT MEANS, you're faithful. It means you care. It means you're there! Being an armor bearer means you're loyal, dependable, reliable, trustworthy, loving and jealous for the honor that is due the subject of interest."

Patty Handly

Exhilarated Service

Several years ago I preached a message entitled, Exhilarated Service. It was during the preparation of this message that I learned that the word service and the word minister are one in the same. Of course my message was on serving because this is one of my favorite subjects and because this was the subject my Pastor asked me to preach. I taught how we are to serve with JOY and EXHILARATION.

Did you know the root word for exhilaration is "hilarity?" Oh my goodness!! When I learned this in my study, I about lost control of all my emotions. I immediately thought of King David. Remember King David danced before the Lord wearing only his linen ephod. King David was "according to his wife, making a fool of himself." KING DAVID WAS OFFERING UP EXHILARATED PRAISE!!

Exhilaration, according to Webster's Dictionary means, to cheer, to gladden, to make merry, to invigorate, to stimulate, to exalt, and TO INSPIRIT … (WHICH IS TO SAY, "to infuse with") spirit or life!" That is awesome!!! "TO INFUSE WITH SPIRIT OR LIFE!!"

I understand now why serving brings me personally such joy, because when I serve, I am being filled with spirit and life!! That makes so much sense to me. That explains why I feel like I am 'at my best' when I am serving. Amen. I'll bet King David felt like he was at his best when he praised the Lord and danced before the Lord with all his might, as we read in 2 Samuel. He may have looked 'a fool' to his wife, but oh I am certain, he did not give a rip what anyone was thinking about him as he was being infused with spirit and with life.

2 Samuel 6:14-15 New King James Version (KJV)

14 Then David danced before the Lord with all his might; and David was wearing a linen ephod. 15 So David and all the house of Israel brought up the ark of the Lord with shouting and with the sound of the trumpet.

In my message, I discussed how we are to serve from a place of humility and love and not a place of pride or anticipation of reward or recognition. We are to serve without limits, hesitation, restraints or conditions. I likened our service unto God to King David's "undignified worship unto the Lord." King David worshipped with hilarious worship, holding nothing back. THIS IS HOW WE SHOULD WORSHIP AND SERVE GOD.

I shared how important it is for each of us to function "together" as the body of Christ. Yes, some are fingers, some hands, some feet, arms and legs, you get the picture. It is only when the Body of Christ functions together "AS ONE BODY" that we will accomplish ALL God has for us to accomplish.

1 Corinthians 12:12 The Message (MSG)

12-13 You can easily enough see how this kind of thing works by looking no further than your own body. Your body has many parts—limbs, organs, cells—but no matter how many parts you can name, you're still one body. It's exactly the same with Christ. By means of his one Spirit, we all said good-bye to our partial and piecemeal lives. We each used to independently call our own shots, but then we entered into a large and integrated life in which he has the final say in everything. (This is what we proclaimed in word and action when we were baptized.) Each of us is now a part of his resurrection body, refreshed and sustained at one fountain—his Spirit—where we all come to drink. The old labels we once used to identify ourselves—labels like Jew or Greek, slave or free—are no longer useful. We need something larger, more comprehensive.

[I RECCOMEND READING ALL OF 1 CORINTHIANS 12:12-30]

"Being an armor bearer isn't always comfortable, it doesn't always feel good. Being an armor bearer doesn't mean your friends or family, IT MEANS, you're faithful. It means you care. It means you're there! Being an armor bearer means you're loyal, dependable, reliable, trustworthy, loving and jealous for the honor that is due the subject of interest."

Patty Handly

Developing the Heart of a Servant

A few years before I had preached the message "Exhilarated Service," my Pastor had lent me a book titled, God's Secret to Greatness, by David Cape and Tommy Tenny. This book changed my life forever. It taught me how we are to minister to others with true humility, (in love) using the power of the towel. In other words, when we humble ourselves and bow our knees to wash the feet of a stranger we are closer than we could ever imagine to developing the heart of Jesus.

When I preached the message on service, I applied the lessons I had learned in the book and I washed the feet of almost everyone in attendance. It was an amazing experience and an unforgettable privilege both to preach and to have been allowed to wash the feet of so many.

[To be honest with you, I didn't know foot washing was sometimes practiced in churches. I thought this was something "new" God had just asked me to do during my lesson. Well, apparently, I was about the only one in the church that night, who did not know this was a normal practice within the church.]

I would love one day to begin to hit the streets of Modesto with a towel in hand and some water in which to wash the feet of anyone who would allow me such a privilege. I know, in God's time, I will do this. I further know this act of foot washing will bless me, more than anyone whose feet I wash. It is an incomprehensive joy to be used in such a way. Until then, I shall continue to look for other ways to bless people, because, I will never cease to desire to be an on purpose blessing.

Choosing to be a Servant

So many of us want to be "MINISTERS OF THE GOSPEL," yet, so few are interested in being servants of the Gospel. We have had it backwards for so long. If we are ever going to minister to anyone, we must first (in the process) serve. In other words, "People DO NOT WANT to hear what we have to say, rather, they want to see what we are willing to do, for them."

Earlier I said, minister and service is the same word. What I should have said is, they are the same by definition. According to Dictionary.com, the word MINISTER means "To give service, to aid, to contribute to (as in comfort)" while the word SERVE means "To be of use, (useful), to aid, to help." With regards to "God," it means "To render obedience, unto God."

I know we are all in process. We are all learning and growing every single day, so, I am happy that there is hope, but I believe some people think when they become ORDAINED ministers, it will be their time to be served. I can tell you this, when we become ordained ministers, the doors to serving others will never close, the clock on the wall will no longer represent ANYTHING AT ALL, and we will be challenged as never before to LIVE (AND LOVE) AS CHRIST. Or, we will fail Him and we will fail others Royally. (Pun intended)

Look at the life of Christ, our example. Jesus did not go around with an attitude desiring servants awaiting His needs. On the contrary, Jesus picked up the towel and washed the feet of His disciples. Jesus waited tables in making sure the multitudes were fed. Jesus provided wine at the wedding at Cana when the original wine was all gone. Jesus always kept the needs of the people ahead of His own.

Matthew 10:45 New King James Version (KJV)

45 For even the Son of Man did not come to be served, but to serve, and to give His life a ransom for many."

It was this heart of ministry, this heart of service that caused Jesus to leave His throne in heaven to come to earth and enter a world of humanity as a child in the womb of young girl who would become his Mother. Jesus, Who already held a position, Who already knew Who He was, came to earth and gave His life that we would know Him and we see His example, His humility, His compassion and His love. Yes, He was AND IS the greatest servant of all. 2000 plus years later, He still bears the scars that show His great love for all humankind.

Becoming "Consider-it"

As armor bearers we are to uphold our Pastors as we uphold the Lord, with the utmost 'consideration.' I say this because when we consider a matter, or think about a person intentionally, or on purpose, we are better able to serve them. Why? Because NOW, we are paying attention. We have made an investment of time and energy and now they matter.

When we are being considerate or 'consider-it,' we will see the needs of others much sooner than when we are not being considerate. When we are consider-it we are able to pray more effectively and with greater compassion and conviction. When we are not being considerate chances are we will not invest our time, prayer or energy into others and they will be "unserved" and neglected.

[We see the concern Christ had with the neglect of others in the Book of Acts. I like to think Christ was being consider-it of the widows and orphans.]

Acts 6:1-4 The Message (MSG)

1-4 During this time, as the disciples were increasing in numbers by leaps and bounds, hard feelings developed among the Greek-speaking believers—"Hellenists"—toward the Hebrew-speaking believers because their widows were being discriminated against in the daily food lines. So the Twelve called a meeting of the disciples. They said, "It wouldn't be right for us to abandon our responsibilities for preaching and teaching the Word of God to help with the care of the poor. So, friends, choose seven men from among you whom everyone trusts, men full of the Holy Spirit and good sense, and we'll assign them this task. Meanwhile, we'll stick to our assigned tasks of prayer and speaking God's Word."

I think it is important to take note that the 12 disciples did not stop the assignment Christ had given them to appease the Hellenists complaints, rather, they appointed others, "trustworthy, proven men," to take on this new task of caring for the widows. I believe this is so important to mention.

[When the Lord gives us an assignment and provides the opportunity, it is imperative that we do not become sidetracked by OTHERS and lose our focus or our vision because we're trying to take on another task given by someone other than the LORD]

There will always be other work to be done. There will always be people who have appointed themselves to direct your steps with perhaps well meaning intentions, but we must never get our eyes off the assignment we have received from the Lord, for therein lies our true destiny. The Lord will provide for the needs of these other tasks or assignments, if they are indeed something He is concerned about. Just as He provided for the widows and orphans, without changing the assignment of the disciples.

I am always encouraged with the provision of the Lord. In the past six years of my life, the Lord has provided for every need of mine, including the provision of cars, for myself, my son and for friends whom we have had the privilege of blessing as well. I'm always puzzled when someone asks me, "Well, how can you afford this?" To which I can only respond, "God is faithful, He keeps blessing me and blessing me and blessing me."

I do believe we must be thankful, mindful and careful with what God entrusts to our care. I know and I believe, when we are faithful with the little He will give us the greater.

Matthew 25:21 Amplified Bible (AMP)

21 His master said to him, Well done, you upright (honorable, admirable) and faithful servant! You have been faithful and trustworthy over a little; I will put you in charge of much. Enter into and share the joy (the delight, the blessedness) which your master enjoys.

I have had both, little and much. I don't mind having little, but it is sure nice to have much. When I am blessed with much I am able to more freely give to others. Now, that is my heart's desire.. to give and give and give and give without ever considering a lack at all BECAUSE God is so faithful to me. He knows I will always give as much as I am able, the more He gives me, the more I give others. THAT'S THE WAY HE LIKES IT.

As armor bearers, we must be considerate of our Pastor's needs. We should not ever allow ourselves to neglect their needs. I can tell you this, the number one need of all Pastors is to be covered in prayer by godly anointed prayer warriors who prefer the position of 'the knee, over the position of the ME.' We must work together, members of one body, steadfast in the service of our Pastors. Never neglecting one another or the needs of the body itself. We should be diligent in the service of others and always abounding in the work of the Lord.

1 Timothy 4:14-16 The Message (MSG)

11-14 Get the word out. Teach all these things. And don't let anyone put you down because you're young. Teach believers with your life: by word, by demeanor, by love, by faith, by integrity. Stay at your post reading Scripture, giving counsel, teaching. And that special gift of ministry you were given when the leaders of the church laid hands on you and prayed—keep that dusted off and in use.

15-16 Cultivate these things. Immerse yourself in them. The people will all see you mature right before their eyes! Keep a firm grasp on both your character and your teaching. Don't be diverted. Just keep at it. Both you and those who hear you will experience salvation.

DID YOU CATCH THAT? VS. 16 ...

"Just keep at it, {for in doing so} BOTH YOU AND THOSE WHO HEAR YOU WILL EXPERIENCE SALVATION!! (Parentheses added)

Make Up Your Mind,
Becoming "On Purpose"

Since the day of my salvation, I have not always lived, moved and had my being in Christ, or even lived "on purpose." I allowed myself to be knocked down and to be derailed many times. I have even made decisions that caused me to fall and caused me to fail assignments. **BUT** God is faithful. When I came to the end of myself, much like the prodigal son, I began to understand I wanted something more in my life, I wanted Someone more. So, I took one step toward Christ and HE took one leap toward me.

I love the story of the Prodigal Son in the Bible. It is found in the Gospel of Luke chapter 15, verses 11-32. In this story a man has two sons. The one son asks his father if he may have his portion (of his goods), then he takes off and lives precariously and squanders all his money and goods leaving him to tend the pigs, which at that time he believed were doing better than him, at least they had food. Scripture tells us he was even willing to eat the pigs food, that's how low he had allowed himself to fall.

Luke 15:16

[16] And he would gladly have filled his stomach with the pods that the swine ate, and no one gave him anything.

The prodigal son FINALLY makes up his mind that he is no longer going to stay away and do without, but rather, decides to return to his father's house and to become a servant, because even the servants are doing better than he is at that moment. So he returns home, humbly and meets his father on the road. The prodigal son has had a heart change and an attitude adjustment to say the least.

Now, I noticed one thing that pops up every time I read this story. While in the pig pen, the prodigal makes a bold statement about returning to his father and becoming one of his father's servants, but upon his return, he never does offer to become a servant to his father.

Luke 15:18

[18] I will arise and go to my father, and will say to him, "Father, I have sinned against heaven and before you, [19] and I am no longer worthy to be called your son. Make me like one of your hired servants."'

At first, I used to think the son kind of cheated, in not offering to become a hired servant. I know he does tell his father he is no longer worthy to be called his son. So, perhaps, his father interrupts him. Perhaps the father realizes what his son is going to say, and seeing his heart of repentance, he simply prevents him from speaking these words. After all, we know the father has been waiting for his son, and he is filled with excitement upon his return, as we continue to read in Luke.

Luke 15:20-24

20 So he got up and came to his [own] father. But while he was still a long way off, his father saw him and was moved with pity and tenderness [for him]; and he ran and embraced him and kissed him [fervently].

21 And the son said to him, Father, I have sinned against heaven and in your sight; I am no longer worthy to be called your son [I no longer deserve to be recognized as a son of yours]!

22 But the father said to his bond servants, Bring quickly the best robe (the festive robe of honor) and put it on him; and give him a ring for his hand and sandals for his feet.(C)

23 And bring out that [wheat-]fattened calf and kill it; and let us revel and feast and be happy and make merry,

24 Because this my son was dead and is alive again; he was lost and is found! And they began to revel and feast and make merry.

Perhaps it was the great display of acceptance and love his father showed that persuaded the son from offering to be his servant.

I choose to believe the son stepped into his position as his father's beloved son. I believe the reason the son never offered to become a servant to the father was because the son had finally received his true inheritance. The inheritance I wrote about earlier in the book, the inheritance of sonship. Yes, the prodigal now knew his identity. He now understood and accepted his father's love. No longer was his identity in his riches, but now his identity was found in his sonship to his father. Upon his return he received the gift and inheritance of sonship and in doing so, he could no longer consider being a hired servant as he had intended, when he was a long way off.

The Choice is Mine

I want to acknowledge the Lord in all things. I choose to be a servant and an armor bearer because I believe that is who I was created to be. I want to an on purpose blessing to everyone I come in contact with every single day of my life. Currently, I know I am not, but with God all things are possible and I believe as long as I never give up and as long as I rely upon God to help me, I will one day hear those beautiful words, "well done Thy good and faithful SERVANT!!"

It is my greatest desire to allow the Lord to operate in me and through me. It is also my great desire that He operates in you and through you. I want to be like Christ and be a servant to all. I don't want to see differences in people, status, race, sick or healthy, rich or poor. I just want to see Jesus in each of His creations and serve them with my whole heart, soul, mind and strength. I want to be Jesus with skin on. Yes, I believe I am a minister (AKA, servant) of the Gospel of Christ, and as such, it is my deep desire to follow in His footsteps.

Although I believe I am called to be a teacher, a preacher, and an evangelist, I choose first and foremost to answer the call to be a servant to all.

The true servant will always remember how it felt to be in the pig pen. He will always remember how it felt to be without friends, food, peace, safety because of the wrong decisions he made. But he will also, always remember that place where the Father ran to Him and held him in His arms and welcomed him home.

The Choice is Yours

It is my sincere desire that you would come to that place today. The Bible says, "Now is the day of salvation."

2 Corinthians 6:2New King James Version (NKJV)

² For He says:

"In an acceptable time I have heard you,

And in the day of salvation I have helped you."

Behold, now is the accepted time; behold, now is the day of salvation.

Beloved friend, the Lord has made a way for you to not only know Him as your Lord and Savior, but also to know Him as your closest friend. He has a great inheritance for you and as you surrender your will to Him He will show you His will for you. I can tell you this, it is a much better plan than you or I could ever imagine.

The Bible says it, so we know it is true.

Jeremiah 29:11-13Amplified Bible (AMP)

¹¹ For I know the thoughts and plans that I have for you, says the Lord, thoughts and plans for welfare and peace and not for evil, to give you hope in your final outcome.

¹² Then you will call upon Me, and you will come and pray to Me, and I will hear and heed you.

¹³ Then you will seek Me, inquire for, and require Me [as a vital necessity] and find Me when you search for Me with all your heart.[4]

This is one of my absolutely favorite Scriptures in the Word of God. It is personal to me. It was one of two Scriptures the Lord first gave to me after I asked Him into my heart. This Scripture made me secure in His plans and in His provision. I may have once lived in the Father's house and then in the pig pen, but now, I am back in the loving arms of my Daddy.

I pray that wherever you are in relationship with the Lord that you will allow Him to be the Lord and Savior of your life. I pray that you will say yes to His decision to adopt you. I pray you will receive your inheritance of sonship and that you will truly become His faithful armor bearer. Remember, we simply surrender to His will and take heed to His Word, and His plans, then, He will do the hard part.

Will you pray with me …

"Yes Lord, I will be Your faithful servant and Your armor bearer. I will humble myself and pray. I will seek Your face, turn from my wicked (selfish) ways and in all things acknowledge You. I receive You (once again) into my heart and ask that You would be my Lord and my Savior. I believe You died on the cross for my sins and that You have plans for me that are good, very good. With Your help, I know we will accomplish all that You desire to do in me and through me. I will submit to the authority of my Pastor and surrender to those You have placed in authority over me. I will pray and encourage them and I will stand with them, and not stand against them. As You have been my example Lord, so I choose now, to follow You in becoming God's Faithful Armor Bearer. I pray as I serve others, they will see my good works and glorify our Father in heaven, so help me God."

"Being an armor bearer isn't always comfortable, it doesn't always feel good. Being an armor bearer doesn't mean your friends or family, IT MEANS, you're faithful. It means you care. It means you're there! Being an armor bearer means you're loyal, dependable, reliable, trustworthy, loving and jealous for the honor that is due the subject of interest."

Patty Handly

Becoming Determined

I believe when you prayed those words, you meant them. I believe your heart is in the perfect place right now for me to encourage you. Becoming an armor bearer takes time, it takes work and it takes patience. Don't beat yourself up when you forget to pray or if you aren't being consider-it. NOTICE IT AND MOVE ON. Believe me, my Pastor can tell you, I have fallen many times with the best of intentions.. I have blown it over and over again. It isn't the falling that counts. It is the getting back up that counts.

[We've heard it again and again, those with great successes also have great failures.]

Did you know that although Kobe Bryant now holds the ALL TIME RECORD for most missed shots in the NBA, (13,418), he has done quite impressively in a few other areas.

Kobe is ranked #3 for ALL TIME MOST POINTS with 32,482

Kobe is ranked #2 for MOST POINTS IN A SINGLE GAME with 81 points, second only to the great Wilt Chamberlin.

And, if you are a baseball fan, you are familiar with the Great Bambino, the Sultan of Swat, Babe Ruth. Did you know that Babe Ruth held four records in one season alone?

Babe Ruth tied the record with A's player, Tillie Walker for THE MOST HOME RUNS, in a single game. (11) In that same year, Ruth had the record for THE MOST STRIKE OUTS!!

Did you know after the Boston Red Sox traded Babe Ruth it took them 86 YEARS to finally win another World Series?

Isn't it interesting that both Kobe and Babe were determined to be the best!! In this effort to be the best, they gave it their all, each game. While some may think Kobe Bryant doesn't like to share, I think he is simply confident that he is doing what he is called and gifted to do and that is to play basketball.

It is my sincere desire that you will allow God the opportunity to use you and keep you in His perfect plan. I pray you will take all of this to heart and truly become His hands and His feet, as you serve others and bring His love to everyone you meet each day.

I cannot say it enough, to everyone who reads this, "Uphold your Pastors, submit to their authority, and humbly serve them as unto the Lord. It is our responsibility to be armor bearers and run with the vision of our Pastors. We must be willing to get this part right. We are called to love one another as Christ loves the Church."

To Whom Much is Given

One day my Pastor shared a word with me, later she shared it with the congregation. She said, "The blessings and favor of God come with great responsibility." That has always stayed in my spirit. I truly believe to whom much is given, much is required.

Those of us blessed and fortunate enough to have Godly, Word-preaching Pastor's understand the difference between meat and milk when it is served from the pulpit. If you're blessed like me, with THAT Pastor, you're also probably very serious about the Word and study. You know that we are VERY RESPONSIBLE!! In the 2,140 days I have attended Soul Harvest Worship Center, I have been fed only the premium of meats and no fat to speak of. It has been served up with all the fixins including (most days) multiple desserts.

I am both privileged and honored that the Lord has allowed me to sit in a house that hosts His presence and honors Him with the greatest of intentions. I pray His presence will ever abide in these temples not made of wood and stone, but in these earthen vessels of honor.

I am humbled that you have completed the reading of this book. I pray with all my heart it has encouraged you to truly make a decision to be a servant to God and man. I pray you have felt my heart and that in some small way I have been a blessing to your life.

Dear friend, I pray the Lord will reveal Himself to you in a brand new way. I pray He will show you new things and new ways you can be an on purpose blessing. I pray you will allow Him to stir you up and quicken you when there is someone in need that He would like you to help. I pray your heart would continue to seek Him and that you will always be on time, on task and on target.

Dedication and Acknowledments

Dear Lord, how can I ever thank You for all You do for me each and every day? I love You so much and I am forever Yours. I pray You will help me to become Your faithful armor bearer. I pray I will be faithful and true till the day I go home to see You face to face. I pray You will make a way for this book to get into the hands of all Your sons who so desire to be ON PURPOSE. I appreciate each and every day You bless me to be a blessing to others.

Now I ask that You will bless my precious Pastor, Verna Brown. Today as I finish this book, I am celebrating her life, her gift, her love for You. Thank You Lord for creating Verna Brown, thank You for creating her in Your image and in Your likeness. Thank You for allowing her to get up each and every time she falls down. Thank You for the armor bearers that surround her both in spirit and in truth.

Today, I honor her, as it is her birthday. I dedicate this book to my Pastor and my beloved friend. I bless her in the mighty name of Jesus. I give You thanks for her dedication to the Word of God and the souls of men. I honor her as a Godly example and I pray You will give her the greatest desire of her heart, which is "to bring You the reward of Your suffering, which is souls."

A Personal Note for My Pastor,

Thank you Pastor Verna for allowing me the privilege of serving you and loving you. Thank you for your patience with me as I fall and get back up . Thank you for loving me enough to correct me and to show me that even when I fall I am not a failure. Oh, I am so thankful to God for the gift you are to my life. You have given your all to me and my family and you have shown me that "love" without works is dead, just like faith without works is dead. You have allowed the Lord to use you in so many ways, my heart is overwhelmed with gratitude. I.S.Y.L.M. yppc-faad=F.A.T. "Happy Birthday, I'm so blessed to have completed the writing of this book at 1:11am on your birthday. It made it that MUCH MORE SPECIAL ... YFAB, PATTY CAKE

In Appreciation

Cynthia, thank you for your gift of photography you were so willing to share in this project so dear to my heart. Your professionalism and your friendship have blessed me more than words can say. I also truly appreciate you taking new author photos. Ha ha.. no one will have to see me in the original shots. I know God healing my body from fibromyalgia helped to make the shot much better. Nobody need ever see the originals. (our little secret) You are such a blessing, thank you.

Pastor Dee Dee Barth, you are such a blessing and such a servant lover. As Pastor Verna's number one warrior (next to Pastor Rick), you demonstrate the heart of a true armor bearer. You blessed me by taking time from your busy schedule to be a part of this book as you allow your feet to be washed. I know not everyone is humble enough to allow his or her feet to be washed by someone else. It actually takes humility and willingness to sit in such a seat of honor. Thank you.

Mojo, (Mavia), thank you so much for being MY ARMOR BEARER MODEL for this book. You are a true young woman of God and I could think of no one more qualified to be on the cover of this book, in the position of the armor bearer... You will grow in the love and humility of the Lord as you continue to love and serve, as you do now. I love how you love me. Thank you for being a part of this very special project.

Johnathen, I am so blessed with your friendship (and Bianca's) I was stoked when you agreed to be my Jesus on the cover. You are a loving, humble man of God whom I admire greatly. I have seen you become more and more like Jesus since you have become a father to Jeremiah. You are a blessing to my heart.

Mary Sherry, thank you for your willingness to help with the initial editing of this book. You are a precious and dear friend whom I am so honored to know. You have been a true servant and freind to so many of us here in the Body. You have been a true support in some of my darkest hours and you have always demonstrated the heart of the Father and the heart of a Mother's love in all you do. My prayers continue for you as you continue to minister to your precious Jim. I appreciate you so much. God bless you.

Kathy, I am so thankful to have you back in my life. I appreciate you helping me with the editing of this book. You were the first person to read this book, besides Pastor Verna. You found most of the errors and the correction with Moses and Abraham really helped. ha ha... I love you dearly and I pray one day I will have the privilege to visit you in Guatamela. Thank you for loving me and blessing me with your friendship. God bless you.

Pastor Rick Brown, I would like to acknowledge and thank you for all you have taught me over these past seven years.

By example, you have shown me what it means to be diligent, hard working, dedicated, loyal, transparent, willing to do the hard stuff, and TRUSTWORTHY. You have proven yourself to be the real deal. You are my true brother and I am blessed to know you are always on my side. Thank you for your consistency and your commitment to excellence. I hope and pray one day we can build more stuff together, and make things beautiful like we did when we worked together on so many different projects. I love you.

Now I would like to acknowledge my previous Pastors, as they are part of the reason I am where I am today.

Pastor Kenny Foreman, thank you for being my very first Pastor. I believe you were the first armor bearer I ever met. You showed me what it means to love the Church, to love the community and to love the Lord with our all. It was so wonderful being a part of Cathedral of Faith, watching God work His miracles through His humble servants. Your vision for the Reaching Out food ministry has never left me. I pray one day I will again be a part of such a ministry, as I was with our "Mission Possible" food ministry in Modesto. I love you Pastor Foreman. Thank you.

Thank you Pastor Mike Garcia for teaching me the importance of KNOWING AND LOVING THE WORD OF GOD. I never forgot the story you shared about why it was so important for you to study to show yourself approved, "a workman who needeth not be ashamed, rightly dividing the Word of truth." After all, "what does it profit a man, if

he gains the whole world and loses his soul, in the process?"
Amen.

Thank you Pastor Ken Foreman Jr. for teaching me the
importance of "loving thy neighbor." I always remembered
when you shared about your neighbor passing away. That
story has never left me, and the Lord even blessed me with a
poem based on this story. I titled it, Preacher Man, Christian
to Christian. Thank you Pastor Ken for all you have done to
bless so many.

To the many Pastors I have had the privilege to listen to,
whether in their churches or via the internet. Thank you for
your uncompromising faith to preach the whole truth and
nothing but the truth, so help you God. There are too many to
name, but I can tell you this.. YOU know who you are, and I
know who you are... and YOU ARE LOVED. THANK YOU
FOR BEING MY FRIENDS. GOD BLESS YOU EACH
AND EVERYONE.I pray you are surrounded by faithful
armor bearers.

Finally, I would like to express my love and gratitude to Dr.
Michelle Corral for allowing me the privilege to sit under
her teaching and serve in her ministry for a brief moment in
time. I am so thankful to you Michelle for teaching me about
the reverential obedient fear of the Lord. You taught me to
love, honor and respect the Holy Spirit and the Anointing of
God Almighty. I learned the importance of honor, and what
it truly means to be an armor bearer by watching you and
observing how you treated the Holy Spirit. Thank you for
being such a true armor bearer to the Lord Jesus Christ. I was

blessed to be associated with Breath of the Spirit Ministries. I am forever thankful for the privilege of joining your team on three missionary trips, back in the day. Thank you so much for these, my first opportunities to be the hands and feet of Jesus. I love you so dearly. God bless you Michelle.

For booking or scheduling speaking engagements please contact Patty Handly personally.

Email: Pattyhandly@yahoo.com

Facebook: user name
Patty Handly

To order books for your church or ministry send email or private Facebook message.

Both **Becoming God's Faithful Armor Bearer** and **My Story, His Glory** are available through email or Facebook. Thank you for your interest. God bless you.

If you desire but cannot afford a copy of the book, please contact Patty personally to discuss possible options.